STATISTICS:
A Guide to Political and Social Issues

HOLDEN-DAY SERIES IN PROBABILITY AND STATISTICS

E. L. Lehmann, Editor

Bickel and Doksum: *Mathematical Statistics*
Carlson: *Statistics*
Freedman: *Markov Processes*
Freedman: *Approximating Countable Markov Chains*
Freedman: *Brownian Motion and Diffusion*
Hájek: *Nonparametric Statistics*
Hodges and Lehmann: *Elements of Finite Probability, 2d ed.*
Hodges and Lehmann: *Basic Concepts of Probability and Statistics,
    2d ed.*
Lehmann: *Nonparametrics: Statistical Methods Based on Ranks*
Nemenyi, Dixon, White: *Statistics From Scratch*
Neveu: *Mathematical Foundations of the Calculus of Probability*
Parzen: *Stochastic Processes*
Rényi: *Foundations of Probability*
*Roberts: *Interactive Data Analysis*
Tanur, Mosteller, Kruskal, et al: *Statistics: A Guide to the Unknown*
Tanur, Mosteller, Kruskal, et al: *Statistics: A Guide to Business
    and Economics*
Tanur, Mosteller, Kruskal, et al: *Statistics: A Guide to Biological
    and Health Sciences*
Tanur, Mosteller, Kruskal, et al: *Statistics: A Guide to Political
    and Social Issues*
*Waller: *Statistics: An Introduction to Numerical Reasoning*

*To be published

STATISTICS: A Guide to Political and Social Issues

by the editors of
STATISTICS: A GUIDE TO THE UNKNOWN

JUDITH M. TANUR
State University of New York, Stony Brook

and

FREDERICK MOSTELLER, Chairman
Harvard University

WILLIAM H. KRUSKAL
University of Chicago

RICHARD F. LINK
Artronic Information Systems, Inc.
and Princeton University

RICHARD S. PIETERS
Phillips Academy, Andover, Mass.

GERALD R. RISING
State University of New York, Buffalo

The Joint Committee on
The Curriculum in Statistics and Probability of
The American Statistical Association and
The National Council of Teachers of Mathematics

and by

E. L. LEHMANN
University of California, Berkeley
Special Editor

ᕼᑯ HOLDEN-DAY, INC.
SAN FRANCISCO   London   Dusseldorf   Johannesburg
Panama   Singapore   Sydney

Copyright © 1977 by Holden-Day, Inc.
500 Sansome Street, San Francisco, California 94111

ISBN   0-8162-8574-8

Library of Congress Catalog Card Number 76-50852

Printed in the United States of America

1234567890   0987

PREFACE

WARREN WEAVER, a great expositor of science, discussed why science is not more widely appreciated and issued a call in "The Imperfections of Science" (*American Scientist*, 49:113, March 1961):

> What we must do—scientists and non-scientists alike—is close the gap. We must bring science back into life as a human enterprise, an enterprise that has at its core the uncertainty, the flexibility, the subjectivity, the sweet unreasonableness, the dependence upon creativity and faith which permit it, when properly understood, to take its place as a friendly and understanding companion to all the rest of life.

As this book makes clear, scientific thinking, most particularly related to statistics, is not restricted to "pure" science, but has many uses in applied fields such as the political and social sciences. And most especially, it is necessary to develop what we might call a statistical attitude toward, and manner of thinking about, these disciplines.

To prepare a volume describing important applications of statistics and probability in many fields of endeavor—this was the project that the ASA-NCTM Committee initiated early in 1969 as an effort to close the gap Weaver and others had pointed out. *Statistics: A Guide to the Unknown* (*SAGTU*) was the result.

During the book's preparation several of us who were working on it and teaching simultaneously found much of the material very useful—even inspirational—to undergraduate and graduate students. It seemed that the book had an additional possible function as an auxiliary textbook. This impression has been confirmed over the years since publication of *SAGTU* as college after college, university after university, and even secondary after secondary school adopted *SAGTU* as an auxiliary textbook for introductory statistics classes.

Instructors and students have reported success in using *SAGTU* as a means of tying techniques and methods, taught necessarily at a simple level with simplified examples, to real problems in the real world. In specialized courses, some teachers wanted sets of essays oriented to their subject matter. Students studying political and social issues, for example, found themselves only distantly concerned with statistical applications in biologic sciences. The very diversity of applications that had fascinated us became an impediment to the usefulness of *SAGTU* as an auxiliary textbook within the time constraints of a specialized statistics course. It is for this reason that the decision was taken to compile what we have come to refer to as mini-*SAGTU*'s: each a selection of articles from *SAGTU* (and in the present and one of the earlier volumes one new article each) dealing with a particular field of application—*Statistics: A Guide to Political and Social Issues* (*SAGPSI*) is the third such volume to appear. (The first two were *SAGBE* and *SAGBAHS*; *Statistics: A Guide*, respectively, *to Business and Economics* and *to Biology and the Health Sciences*.)

The essays here, and in *SAGTU* itself, do not teach technical methods, but rather illustrate past accomplishments and current uses of statistics and probability. In choosing the actual essays to include, the Committee aimed at illustrating a variety of applications, but did not attempt the impossible task of covering all possible uses. Even in the areas included, attempts at complete coverage have been deliberately avoided. We discouraged authors from writing essays that could be entitled "All Uses of Statistics in . . . " Rather, we asked authors to stress one or a very few important problems within their field of application and to explain how statistics and probability help to solve them and why the solutions are useful to the nation, to science, or to the people who originally posed the problem. In the past, for those who were unable to cope with very technical material, such essays have been hard to find.

When describing work in the mathematical sciences, one must make a major decision as to what level of mathematics to ask of the reader. Although the Joint Committee serves professional organizations whose subject matter is strongly mathematical, we decided to explain statistical ideas and contributions without dwelling on their mathematical aspects. This was a bold stroke, and our authors were surprised that we largely held firm.

There is an old saw that a camel is a horse put together by a committee. Our authors supplied exceedingly well-formed and attractive anatomical parts, but to the extent that this book gaits well, credit is due primarily to a most talented and dedicated Committee. In general, the approach to unanimity in the Committee's critical reviews of and suggestions about essays was phenomenal. And, though they may have occasionally been divided about the strong and weak points of a particular essay, they were constantly united in their purpose of producing a useful book, and in their ability to find something more than 24 hours a day to work on it. This dedication undoubtedly created difficulties for our authors. Nevertheless, our authors persevered and deserve enormous thanks from us, and from the Committee, and from the statistical profession at large.

Our thanks go also to the Sloan Foundation whose grant made it possible to put this book together.

There are others to thank as well: to the office of the American Statistical Association (and, in particular, to Edgar Bisgyer, and John

Lehmann, and later Fred Leone) for invaluable help in all the administrative work necessary to get out a book such as this; and similar thanks to the administration of the National Council of Teachers of Mathematics; to Edward Millman for careful and imaginative editorial assistance; and to other people at Holden-Day, especially Frederick H. Murphy, and Erich Lehmann, our Series Editor; to Mrs. Holly Grano for acting as a long-distance and long-haul secretary; and to the many friends and colleagues both of the Editor and of the Committee members who so often acted as unsung, but indispensable, advisors.

In this new effort to compile *SAGPSI*, additional thanks go to the original Committee members and to the guiding spirit of Erich Lehmann. We also have additional thanks for John P. Gilbert, Richard J. Light, and Frederick Mosteller, the authors of the one new article appearing in this volume, "How well do social innovations work?" The supplementary material for study, prepared especially for *SAGBE*, is the valuable contribution of Donna and Leland Neuberg.

Frederick Mosteller
Judith Tanur

Atlanta, Georgia
October, 1975

CONTENTS

MEASURING SOCIOPOLITICAL INEQUALITY

Hayward R. Alker, Jr.   *Massachusetts Institute of Technology*

EQUALITY OR its absence has long been a focal concept in political philosophy. Aristotle spoke against the democratic conception of justice defined as "the enjoyment of arithmetical equality," preferring the enjoyment of proportional equality on the basis of merit or property; in effect he took a conservative, inegalitarian view.   In the spirit of the French Revolution and its radical emphasis on "Liberty, Equality, and Fraternity," Thomas Paine argued that "inequality of rights has been the cause of all the disturbances, insurrections, and civil wars, that ever happened . . . ."

More contemporary discussions often implicitly or explicitly rely on definitions of equality.   The U.S. Constitution calls for "equal protection" under the law.   Citizens of various persuasions argue for or against racial imbalance in their schools, for or against more progressive tax structures.   When sufficiently general questions are asked, the great majority of the American people is for "equality of economic opportunity" and against government by or for a privileged few.   In an historic 1964 decision against legislative malapportion-

1

ment (*Reynolds versus Sims,* 1964), Chief Justice Warren enunciated "the fundamental principle of representation for equal numbers of people, without regard to race, sex, economic status or place of residence within the state."[1]

THE CONTRIBUTION OF DESCRIPTIVE STATISTICS

Of course, statistics cannot in and of itself resolve the moral and political issues raised in these quotations, nor, without the explanatory theories and data of social science, can it answer the many rival claims about the causes and consequences of various kinds of inequality. But I would like to argue that as a set of ideas and practices, statistics has contributed to the clarification of the meanings of sociopolitical *inequality.* In a sense, this achievement amounts to providing a common notion of sociopolitical inequality, several measures or quantitative descriptions of the extent of inequality in a particular situation, and several criteria for choosing one measure over another as more appropriate to a particular situation or concept. After a brief review of some conventional aspects of most statistical measures of inequality, we shall present some of these measures and several criteria for choice among them.

Can we think of such modest statistical accomplishments as in any way a political success? Plato would have considered the formal ideal of justice of ultimate significance, its realization, even imperfectly in the world of politics, a noble human achievement. But is greater sociopolitical equality always greater justice? For Tom Paine it often was, for Aristotle it clearly was not. Evaluations of contemporary progress toward greater political equality or toward multiracial equality of educational opportunity are questions on which citizens disagree. Many would see such achievements as realizations of ideals of equality whose time has come, others as victories for hollow formalisms. Statistical assessments of two such controversial achievements will conclude this paper.

STATISTICAL CONVENTIONS IN MEASURING INEQUALITY

The simplest but perhaps the most important choice that statistical treatments of inequality have conventionally made is to focus on the distribution of valued objects, events, and relationships. These have included income, land, votes, legal treatment, ownership shares, and racially equivalent classmates. The abstractness of the concept of value distribution means that all these different values can be discussed in the same statistical terms.

Does this focus on value distributions seem an obvious or inevitable choice? To some, familiar with notions of income inequality, the answer may be yes. But some deeper reflection suggests that more subjective, more qualitative, and less comparable aspects of inequality might have been focused on. What

[1] This and subsequent citations of the Supreme Court decisions are from *The New York Times,* June 16, 1964, pp. 28–31.

did it mean, for example, to many of the suburban and black voters who were underrepresented in their state legislatures before the major reapportionment decisions of the Supreme Court? Obviously it meant more to some than to others. Except for the common facts of underrepresentation, these meanings were different for many citizens and would be hard to summarize. The same point could be made about income differences, of course. For some, an extra $5000 income would mean being able to pay urgent medical bills; for others, being able to pay for part of their son's college education, a new car, or a pleasure trip to the Taj Mahal.

Nonetheless, the statistical orientation has focused on quantitative common denominators of meaning—a vote is a vote, a dollar a dollar. This interpretation has increased the possibility of comparisons across individuals, families, cities, states, even if it has lost significant subjective differences. Equality before the law or equality of opportunity means something concrete and comparable: similar treatment in similar circumstances.

Another aspect of most serious statistical measures of inequality is that they are, or they rely on, cumulative measures. Thus, in the interests of comparison, a statistician typically looks at the cumulative effects of inequalities in value distribution over an entire population or measures one person's privileged position in terms of how far it is above the average calculated for the whole population. Comparing the largest and the smallest incomes, for example, might make good newspaper copy, but it would not reflect the cumulative impact of the inequalities involved.

In part because of their reliance on cumulative terms, most descriptive statistical measures of inequality are calculated in generally comparable units. Thus a statistician would want to be able to compare income distributions in rubles with those in francs or dollars; to do so he relies on his knowledge of total incomes in each society. Of the several ways of getting such measures, two cumulative procedures will be used frequently here: working with data in percentage and percentile form, and defining indexes on a 0-to-1 or 0-to-100 scale by dividing the raw numerical value in particular units by its maximum value calculated in these same units. The resulting measures are pure numbers; certainly this property maximizes the possibility of comparison across variables.

SEVERAL MEASURES OF SOCIOPOLITICAL INEQUALITY

In a condensed, but geometrically intuitive, way, Figure 1 suggests at least six different but related cumulative measures of sociopolitical inequality. The data there represent the distribution of 150 seats in the New York State Assembly over a total state population of 17 million around 1960. In drawing Figure 1(a), the various Assembly districts (which have one representative each) were ordered from the largest to the smallest in population size. Because each district, regardless of population, elects one assemblyman, it follows

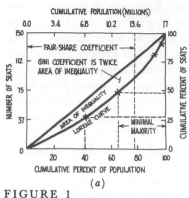
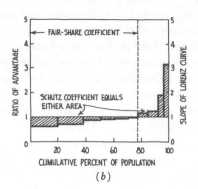

FIGURE 1

*Legislative malapportionment in
the New York State Assembly,
1960. Source: Alker (1965)*

that the most populous districts are the most underrepresented. Plotting the
cumulative percentage of seats controlled by the most underrepresented 10,
20, 30, 40, . . . , 100% of the population and then drawing a smooth curve
through these points gives us our first cumulative measure of inequality: the
Lorenz curve.   Let us draw a vertical line from 40% on the horizontal axis
to the curve, and from there a horizontal line to the right-hand vertical axis.
The reading there shows us that the most underrepresented 40% of the population of New York in 1960 controlled only about 28% of the Assembly seats.
Note that if representation were equally distributed the Lorenz curve would
take the form of a straight line from the lower left corner to the upper
right one, a 45° line.

The Lorenz curve also gives us a second measure of inequality: the percentage of the total held by the most "overrepresented" $n\%$ of the population
(where n may be 1, 5, 8, 10, etc.).   Thus Figure 1(a) shows that the most
"overrepresented" 8% of the population elected 20% of the State Assemblymen!   Going slightly further down the Lorenz curve gives us evidence that
35% of the state's voting population were potentially, through their representatives, a minimal majority in the Assembly.

Leaving Figure 1(a) for a moment, we realize that it has become convenient to talk about "over-" and "under-" represented citizens.   A remarkable
property of the Lorenz cumulative curve is that its slope (inclination, or
rate of increase) provides us with a measure of this "over-" or "under-"
representation.   Figure 1(b), a "slope curve," is in fact a plot of the slope
of the Lorenz curve shown in (a).   To construct the slope curve the data
are grouped into ten 15-seat categories.   The "ratios of advantage" plotted
vertically in (b) show, for example, that the most overrepresented 3.1% of

the population, with 15 Assemblymen, elected more than three times as many representatives as the same number of "average" citizens. For this group the value of the slope—their ratio of advantage in the bar graph (b)—is about 3.2. (A little reflection suggests that this is derivable as follows: if 3.1% of the population elects 15 Assemblymen when an "average" 10% should do so in an Assembly of 150 members, their ratio of advantage is $10/3.1 = 3.2$.)

Another quantitative measure of inequality, comparable across states, is immediately suggested by the slope curve. The *equal-share,* or *fair-share, coefficient* measures what percentage of the population gets less than its equal or fair share of representatives. In New York in 1960, it was 77% for the State Assembly. In other words, 77% of the New York citizen population was at least somewhat underrepresented!

Finally, we come to two summary measures most preferred by statistically minded social scientists, the *Gini coefficient* and the *Schutz coefficient.* The Gini coefficient is the area of inequality [between the ideal 45° line and the actual Lorenz curve in Figure 1(a)] divided by the maximum possible area. This area of inequality ranges from 0 in the case of perfect equality (the poorest 50% of the population still get 50% of the values) to $\frac{1}{2}$ (when an infinitesimally small fraction of the population possesses all the values and the resulting area is the right triangle below the 45° line with sides of 100 and 100). Thus the Gini coefficient itself ranges between 0 and $\frac{1}{2}/\frac{1}{2} = 1$. For the data in Figure 1, a Gini coefficient of 0.22 indicates that malapportionment was 22% of its theoretical maximum value.

Another geometrically appealing measure comes from Figure 1(b). Here we sum the area of advantage above the fair-share coefficient or the area of disadvantage below it. The Schutz coefficient is equal to either the total area of advantage or the total area of disadvantage. It is found by summing the areas of the rectangles to the left of the fair-share coefficient or alternatively by summing the areas of the rectangles to the right of the fair-share coefficient. For the Schutz coefficient, the minimum is obviously zero; its maximum is 1.0 (or 100.0 in percentage units). The New York data give a value of 0.156, or 15.6% for the Schutz coefficient.

All of the measures we have mentioned are in some sense aspects of cumulative quantitative value distributions. Typically they measure deviations from an ideal of perfect equality: a 45° Lorenz curve or a constant ratio of advantage equal to 1.0. But Aristotle and others would not accept the notion of perfect numerical equality. For cases such as income distribution, malapportionment, or more controversially, racial imbalance, they might argue that an appropriate ideal was less than complete equality. We might consider as inequitably or unjustly treated only those taxpayers with incomes below one-third of the national average, only those citizens with ratios of voting advantage below 0.90, or only those students with 25% fewer white classmates than the city average.   In such cases, we could draw Lorenz curves showing maximum allowable inequality as a standard rather than the traditional 45° line.   Slope curves could be derived from such curves, and departures beyond even these lines would then be the basis for a whole class of new cumulative measures of unacceptable inequality.

CRITERIA FOR CHOOSING AMONG MEASURES

Whether defined in egalitarian or inegalitarian terms, two important criteria argue in favor of some version of either the Gini coefficient or the Schutz coefficient.   First of all, each is a full information measure in that all the data are used in calculating them, not just the top 8, 10, 20, or 50%.   Second, if we assume that each datum is as significant as any other, we want measures that are sensitive to all sorts of differences among them.   The minimal majority and fair-share coefficients depend wholly on the location of one point on the Lorenz curve or its slope, but the Gini and Schutz coefficients depend upon location and slope all along the Lorenz curve.   More sensational measures such as "the top 1%, who have such and such . . . " can be misleading as to where the rest of the population stands.

A third criterion for choosing among measures, one offered by Yntema for the study of income inequalities, is the stability of a measure's results when different ways of grouping the data are employed.   Although this may seem a technical criterion of little substantive import, for those often accustomed to getting incomplete data grouped by deciles or quartiles this criterion is an important one in practice.

Another question raised by social statisticians is whether various measures are highly intercorrelated or not.   The implicit criterion is that one needs as many measures of inequality as there are philosophically important and empirically distinct aspects of the phenomenon at hand.   It is of particular interest in the malapportionment case, for example, that both the Gini and the Schutz coefficients give very similar, or highly interrelated, results, with the minimal majority measure not far behind.   That the fair-share coefficient is much less closely related to any of these coefficients argues for the necessity of thinking in terms of additional important and meaningful aspects of any unequal value distribution.

SOME APPLICATIONS OF STATISTICAL MEASURES

Let us briefly discuss two areas of statistical applications, malapportionment and racial imbalance, and close with some speculations about our initial quotation from Thomas Paine.   Although we shall only sketch some of the more interesting findings and the extent to which controversial political achievements have grown from them, it may suffice to convey to the reader the utility of the above conventions, criteria, and measures.

First, a word is in order about New York malapportionment as it was treated by the U.S. Supreme Court. This is perhaps the clearest case of the motivating force of the quantitative equalitarian ideal—the Lorenz line of full equality—stated in "one man, one vote" terms. The close correspondence of the popular minimal majority measures with the more technically adequate Gini and Schutz coefficients in reflecting an underlying reality was seen by the majority of judges in their historic judgment that there was a violation of the Constitutional call for "equal protection" and "the right to vote." Although explicit use of such sophisticated measures is not indicated in the Court's opinion, it is clear that their opinions on *Reynolds versus Sims* reflect statistical perspectives. Even in dissent, Justice Stewart argues that "nobody has been deprived of the right to have his vote counted," while the Warren majority opinion states in quantitative language that "diluting the weight of votes because of place of residence impairs basic right under the 14th Amendment." In language remarkably like the measures we have reviewed, the majority objected to "minority control of state legislative bodies," did not believe that one person ought to "be given twice or ten times the voting power of another," and sympathized when 56% of the citizen population elected only 48% of the Assembly. Realizing that New York in 1960 was less malapportioned than most other American states in terms of the Gini, Schutz, or minimal majority coefficients, we gain some idea of the reenfranchisement that has taken place since then because of the Court's decision. This effort has not been undisputed, however; almost a majority of state legislatures have called for a Constitutional Convention on the reapportionment issue.

Table 1 and the derivative Lorenz curve in Figure 2 show how the Lorenz curve idea can be extended from the cases of income inequality and malapportionment to measure racial imbalance. The cumulative "value" represented in Figure 2 is the percentage of white students available as schoolmates; an analogous figure could have been drawn with percentages of nonwhites. Note that in this case the complete-imbalance picture we described earlier would be impossible unless there were only one white student in all of New Haven. So in order to evaluate the amount of imbalance we have, we must compare the actual Lorenz curve with the one we would have if there were complete imbalance given the existing number of white students. If we were not constrained at all by the sizes of the existing schools, then we could visualize complete imbalance as all of the black students going to all-black schools and all of the white students going to all-white schools. If we then ordered the schools by percentage of white students, we would have a Lorenz curve showing a maximum feasible imbalance that was at first completely flat along the horizontal axis and then slanted up directly to the upper right-hand corner. Because there were four junior high schools in New Haven in 1964 and because these schools had fixed capacities, it is not possible to visualize all the schools as completely segregated; we must have at least one integrated

TABLE 1. The Actual Racial Breakdown of Students in New Haven's Four Junior High Schools, June 1964*

SCHOOLS	NUMBER OF STUDENTS			PERCENTAGES				
	Whites	Non-whites	Total	Percent of All Whites	Percent of All Students	Cumulated Percent of All Whites	Cumulated Percent of All Students	Ratio: Percent Whites/ Percent Students
Bassett	55	555	610	3	17	3	17	0.18
Troup	419	514	933	19	27	22	44	0.70
Sheridan	741	148	889	34	25	56	69	1.36
Fair Haven	968	140	1108	44	31	100	100	1.42
Total	2183	1357	3540	100	100			1.0 (weighted average)

* These data are taken from a document issued by the New Haven Public Schools, Dr. Laurence G. Paquin, Superintendent, June 8, 1964, entitled *Proposals for Promoting Equality of Educational Opportunity and Dealing with the Problems of Racial Imbalance*, pp. 10–11.

8

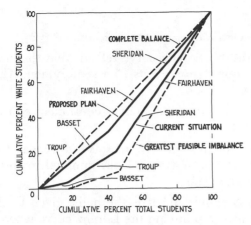

FIGURE 2

Four alternative patterns of racial imbalance in New Haven junior high schools. Source: Alker (1965)

school. Thus the curve of greatest possible imbalance is the lowest one in Figure 2. The actual racial imbalance in the system was measured by a Gini coefficient of 0.25; the maximum possible was 0.40.

Was the cumulative inequality evident in Table 1 and summarized graphically in Figure 2 sufficiently motivating to inspire desirable political action? Of what sort? The New Haven Superintendent proposed, through rezoning and selective busing, to improve racial balance to the considerable extent indicated in Figure 2. The proposed plan would reduce the Gini measure of imbalance from 0.25 to 0.09. After considerable controversy, a somewhat revised plan was evidently put into effect. Many Americans, excluding the majority of the Supreme Court, do not find racial imbalance a compelling issue, so the extent to which such action was a "success" is perhaps more controversial than state legislative reapportionment.

Finally, let us consider some inequalities that have inspired little or no "successful" political action. Recall that Thomas Paine claimed that inequality of rights "has been the cause of all civil insurrections." Statistical analyses do show land and income inequalities within nations to contribute to domestic group violence.

Whether the more extreme and growing inequality between the rich and poor nations of the world has or will occasion similar violence or corrective action remains an open question. Do the members of the poorer, mostly non-white, relatively powerless majority of the world's population have a right to a better life or to more control over their destiny? The answer lies in the success or failure of a revolutionary statistical ideal.

PROBLEMS

1. What is the advantage of a *cumulative* measure of inequality?

2. Consider Figure 1. Suppose the Lorenz curve tells us that the most under-represented 18% of the population elects 15 assemblymen. What is the "ratio of advantage" of this group?

3. Why are the two ways of computing the Schutz coefficient equivalent? (Hint: Refer to Figure 1b.)

4. What is the minimal majority? In Figure 1a, why is it drawn at 49% rather than 51% of the Assembly seats? (Hint: Does minimal majority refer to over- or under- representation?)

5. Study Figures 1a and 1b *together*. What is the name given to the percentage of the population at the point on the Lorenz curve where a tangent of the curve is parallel to the 45° line? (Hint: What is the slope of the 45° line?)

6. What is the major advantage of both the Gini and Schutz coefficients?

7. Explain what is meant by a *summary* (or *full information*) measure of inequality. Of the six measures of inequality the author discusses, which two are summary measures?

8. Consider Table 1.
    (a) What percentage of the students at Fair Haven were non-white?
    (b) What percentage of all non-white students attended Sheridan?

9. (a) Draw the Lorenz curve for *complete* imbalance for Figure 2.
    (b) What is the value for the "area of inequality" in this case?
    (c) Roughly what percentage of the students in a situation of complete imbalance are white?

10. Refer to Figure 2. (Give approximate answers.)
    (a) Using the "proposed plan" curve for Basset and Troup (taken together), what is the cumulative percentage of white students? Of total students?
    (b) Using the "greatest feasible imbalance" curve, what is the cumulative percentage of white students at Basset? At Troup?
    (c) Using the "current situation" curve, what percentage of all white students attend Troup? (Check your answer with Table 1.)

REFERENCES

H. R. Alker, Jr.   1965.   *Mathematics and Politics*.   New York: Macmillan.

H. R. Alker, Jr. and B. M. Russett.   1966.   "On Measuring Inequality."   R. Merrit and S. Rokkan, eds., *Comparing Nations*.   New Haven, Conn.: Yale.   Pp. 349–382.

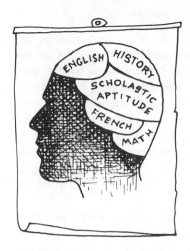

CALIBRATING COLLEGE BOARD SCORES*

William H. Angoff   *Educational Testing Service*

MOST DIRECTORS of testing programs are reluctant to use the same form (edition) at different administrations of a mental test and prefer instead to introduce different forms at different times.   Their reluctance is understandable. Continued reuse of the same form encourages the collection of files of test questions and makes it possible for some students to acquaint themselves in advance with the questions that will later appear on the test.   This practice not only invalidates their performance on the test, but it clearly works to the unfair disadvantage of those students who have not had access to the items.   There are other problems too.   For example, the measurement of growth, practice, fatigue, and so on, which require two or more administrations of a test, is often

* The present article draws heavily upon "How We Calibrate College Board Scores," which the author published in *The College Board Review,* No. 68, (Summer) 1968. We express our appreciation to the College Entrance Examinations Board for their permission to publish this revision.

rendered infeasible because the second measurement is contaminated by the student's recollection of the questions he was exposed to at the time of the first testing. Although many such problems can be circumvented by the practice of using different test forms at different administrations, this practice brings with it other problems that also require solution. In any testing program which makes use of a number of different forms of the same mental test there will inevitably be variations in difficulty from form to form. Therefore, if the scores of individuals who take the different forms are to be compared with one another for the evaluation of their relative abilities, it is necessary in the interests of equity to calibrate, or "equate," the scores on the different forms.

The process of equating is a statistical one which in our testing programs at Educational Testing Service (ETS) ultimately yields an equation for converting raw scores to scaled scores. Thus, except for random error, one can assume that a student who has earned a scaled score of, say, 563 on a particular test form would have earned that same scaled score whether he had taken a more difficult or less difficult form of the test than the one he actually took. That is, the score of 563 that is reported to him is *his* score and represents *his* level of performance (and, by inference, his level of ability) at the time that he took the test.

More generally speaking, the score of 563 represents a particular level of ability—let us say, verbal ability as measured by the verbal section of the Scholastic Aptitude Test (SAT)—in the same sense that the measurement 62°F represents a measurement (much more precise, of course) of temperature. It is a measurement which is independent of the type of Fahrenheit thermometer used, the time of year in which the measurement was taken, or the temperatures of other places in the world at the time. Similarly, the score of 563 is taken to represent the same level of ability, whoever earns it, in the same sense that 62°F represents the same degree of temperature, whether the object measured is air, water, coffee, or a martini.

THE MEANING OF SCORES

The questions are sometimes asked "What does the score signify? Is it high or is it low? How far is it above the average?" Once again, the temperature analogy is appropriate because the same questions may be asked with respect to the measurement of 62°F: "What does 62° mean? Is it warm or is it cool? How close is it to the average?" It needs little elaboration to say that these questions cannot be answered as they are stated. Sixty-two degrees represents a high temperature when compared with mean temperatures in New York City in January; it represents a low temperature when compared with mean temperatures in New York in July. At any given time it is warm compared with temperatures at the poles, but cool compared with most temperatures at the equator. It is cool for acceptable morning coffee and, most experts will agree, intolerably warm for a martini. Similarly, 563 is high or low, promising or disappointing, acceptable or unacceptable, depending on the choice of the particular reference group and on the standards set in the educational endeavor to which the student aspires.

The question that *should* be asked in interpreting scores is "How does this student compare with other students who are competing with him?" or, more fundamentally, "Is it possible to compare this student with other students, even though they may not all have been measured with precisely the same form of the test?"

Viewed slightly differently, the purpose of equating is to maintain a constant scale over time in the face of changing test forms and different kinds of students. Only if this purpose is achieved will it be possible to compare students tested today with students tested five years ago, to plot trends, and to draw conclusions regarding, for example, the effects of practice, the effects of growth, the effects of changing curricula, or the effects of changes in the composition of the student group over the course of time.

CONSTANCY OF SAT SCALED SCORES

One popular misconception is that SAT scaled scores, which are expressed on a 200–800 scale, are reported "on a curve," separately defined and separately determined at each administration of the test. This type of scaling is intentionally *not* carried out. For if it were, it would be impossible to compare students tested at different administrations, since the average scaled score for all administrations, by definition, would be the same. Moreover, under such a system a student's scaled score would depend in part on the caliber of the group with which he happened to take the test. It would be to his advantage, therefore, to take the test with a generally lower-scoring group, because he would stand relatively high in comparison with that group, and would consequently receive a higher score than if he were to take the test with a higher-scoring group. The scale that is used in the College Board program (among others) is a constant scale, defined once and *only* once, and perpetuated in that form from that time on.

To do this we construct for each form of a test an equation by which raw scores on a test form are converted to scaled scores. The methods that are followed in the equating process are so designed as to produce an equation that is *characteristic of the test form itself* and relatively unaffected by the nature of the group of individuals on whom the data were collected to form the basis of the equating process.

The equating of raw scores on two forms of a test requires an assessment of the relative difficulty of those forms. This requirement implies that ideally the same group of individuals should take both forms. But because the data for equating are drawn from operational administrations at which only one form is administered to each student, two separate groups of students must be chosen for analysis, one group taking one of the two forms and the other group taking the second. However, these two groups are likely to be different, with respect to both average ability and dispersion (spread) of ability. Therefore, any evaluation of the relative difficulties of the forms on the basis of a direct examination of the data for these two groups could well be misleading and biased. Such an evaluation could easily result in a conversion equation for Form X that is contaminated by the characteristics of the groups rather than one that is based solely on the characteristics of the test forms. For example, if the group taking Form X is brighter, we might erroneously decide that Form X is easier. Some means, therefore, is needed to adjust for differences between the two groups.

The device used for making these adjustments is a short "equating" test administered to both groups, A and B, at the time that they take the regular operational test. Sometimes the equating test is a separately timed test administered during the course of the testing session; sometimes it is not a separate test at all, but instead, a collection of questions interspersed throughout the operational test. This collection of questions, nevertheless, is treated statistically as though it were a separate test. At the time that the equating of the operational forms (Forms X and Y) is carried out, scores are derived for the two groups on *both* the equating test *and* the operational forms that were administered to them. Appropriate formulas are then applied to the statistics observed for the two groups to yield estimates of the behavior of the two forms as though they had been administered to the same group.

If the equating test is to be used as a basis for comparing the two groups and making adjustments for differences between them, then it must represent precisely the same test for both groups. The restrictions are easy to satisfy when the equating test is separately timed; in most instances a separately timed equating test and its directions need only to be reprinted.

The restrictions are not so easily satisfied, however, when the equating test is a collection of individual questions interspersed throughout the test. Here special care must be taken to avoid differential contextual effects. For example, questions such as those in reading comprehension or data interpretation sections (questions that pertain to a single passage or to a single graph or set of numerical data) should ordinarily be used as a block because there is a real possibility that they will be interdependent. If they are, any change in the composition of the block could well disturb the meaning of the individual questions. Matching questions (e.g., questions that call for matching people with events, works, philosophies) must be taken as a group. Care should also be taken to put the equating questions in one form in about the same relative position as in the other form. It is advisable to avoid using equating questions that appear near the end of the test, where failure to answer the questions may be caused as much by insufficient time to respond to them as by their inherent difficulty.

The conversion equation for a test form provides a description of its overall difficulty and discriminating power because it essentially "locates" or "places" the test form on the scaled-score scale. For example, if a test form is relatively easy, then the scaled score corresponding to a given raw score will be lower than the corresponding scaled score on a more difficult form. A score of 57, for example, on an easy test form might correspond to a scaled score of 590. On a more difficult form the very same raw score of 57 might correspond to a scaled score of 640. Obviously, the score of 640 can be earned on the easier form only by getting a raw score higher than 57. This result is intuitively equitable, since the successful completion of 57 difficult questions *merits* a higher scaled score than the successful completion of 57 easy questions.

SCALING ACHIEVEMENT TEST SCORES

The foregoing discussion dealt with the problem of adjusting the scores on alternate and interchangeable forms of a test, so that a person of given ability will earn the same scaled score regardless of the form of the test he happens to have taken. The type of solution that is given here is appropriate to the problem that we face when, for example, we wish to compare or merge data for individuals or groups of individuals who have taken different forms of the same test. From a theoretical point of view, at least, this is a relatively simple problem. The problem is different and far more complex, however, when we wish to compare two individuals (or groups) who have taken entirely different tests, for example, in chemistry and in French.

Of course, from a logical or educational point of view it makes no sense to compare the scores of two individuals who have taken entirely different tests. But like it or not, such comparisons are inevitable, and logical or not, they are made. Just as the grade-point average is a composite of marks earned by different students in different combinations of courses and just as it is used for comparing and evaluating the relative accomplishments of different individuals (e.g., for determining pass, fail, and honor status), scores on different Achievement Tests are also compared, merged, averaged, and ranked in many college admissions offices as they must be. Recognizing as a fact of life that incomparable things *will* be compared, it behooves us to construct a system that, while it cannot be wholly satisfactory, will represent an improvement in the status quo and avoid some of its obvious imperfections. The problem and its solution are as follows.

In the College Board Admissions Testing Program, all candidates typically take the Scholastic Aptitude Test. No option is given. In the Achievement Test series, however, there are options. Candidates may take one, two, or three of the 16 Achievement Tests in the series; moreover, they may take any one, two, or three they feel inclined or prepared to take. Therefore, while virtually all candidates take the SAT, the group of candidates taking any

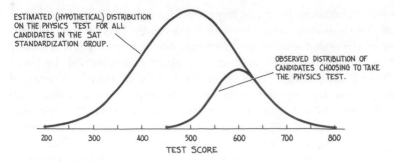

FIGURE 1

Hypothetical distribution of physics test scores for everyone and for students electing to take the physics test. Source: Angoff (1968)

one of the Achievement Tests is a self-selected group, each one different from the next in overall level and dispersion of ability. The problem arises when we wish to compare the scores of the groups of students who take different Achievement Tests.

In order to make these comparisons more equitably, the system of scores reported for the various Achievement Tests (which all use the same 200–800 score scale used for the SAT) is constructed to reflect the level and dispersion of abilities (as measured by the SAT) of the students who characteristically take each of the tests. The statistical process that results in this type of scale construction involves making an estimate of the performance on each Achievement Test of the entire original College Board standardization group for the SAT, assuming that they all had the appropriate instruction in the subject and all took the test. As a result, the scores for a test such as the physics test, which is typically taken by a relatively high-scoring segment of all the candidates who take the SAT, are automatically "placed" relatively high on the scale. Correspondingly, the scores for a test which is typically taken by a low-scoring segment of all the candidates who take the SAT are "placed" relatively low on the scale. A schematic diagram describing the distribution of scores on the physics test for *all* candidates taking the SAT and also for those choosing to take the physics test appears in Figure 1.

PURPOSE OF SCALING

The purpose of this type of scaling is to ensure that a candidate who chooses to compete with more able candidates is not put at a disadvantage, that is, that a candidate who is average in a highly selected group of candidates will earn a higher scaled score than a candidate who is average in a less able group. The intent is to make it impossible for a candidate to "beat the game" by taking advantage of the machinery of the testing program and making a *strategic* choice of the particular Achievement Test (or tests) that will yield the highest score(s) for him.   Moreover, since the scores on the various tests are scaled in accordance with the abilities of the candidates who typically choose to take them, it is possible for college admissions officers to take an average of the scores offered by each candidate with relative confidence that the average represents an equitable basis for comparing students who have taken different combinations of tests.

Given, then, that there are wide variations in the ability levels (and dispersions) of the groups of candidates taking the various tests, and given also that the scales for the tests reflect these variations, one would expect that the highest possible scaled scores on the various tests would vary substantially and systematically from test to test. As a result, it would be possible for an able student of physics to earn a higher scaled score than an equally able student of a subject that is generally chosen by less able students, simply because the scale for the physics test permitted it.   In order, then, to equalize the opportunities for high scores among the different subgroups of candidates, the maximum score of 800 is imposed across the board for all tests, and the test specifications for each of the Achievement Tests are so written as to ensure, as nearly as possible, that a score of 800 may be achieved on every test and on every form.   Similarly, the minimum score of 200 is imposed across the board for all tests; any raw score that would ordinarily "scale out" below 200 is reported as 200.   However, because precise discriminations in the vicinity of 200 are not as often necessary on the Achievement Tests, there is no corresponding effort to ensure that a score of 200 is possible on every test.   The 200 and 800 limits simply mean that scores are not reported *beyond* those limits.   The principal reasons for having them are: (1) as already indicated, to minimize *gross inequities* across the test offerings, and (2) to make it clear that the tests can discriminate adequately only within a limited range of scaled scores.

NECESSITY FOR REFINED SCORES

For the most part, the processes of equating and scaling the scores for College Board tests produce effects of relatively small magnitude, and thus they could be regarded as only a pedantic refinement.   But that is not so.   They are a refinement of a basic sort, introduced to ensure that no student will be put either to an advantage or a disadvantage simply because he happened to have taken an easier or more difficult form of the test or because he happened to have taken the test with a less able or more able group of students.

Fundamentally, what is desired is a measurement of ability that will serve the best interests of the students, a measurement that is not only accurate and relevant for them, but also, and just as importantly, equitable.   It is to this goal of equity that the "refinement" of equating and scaling is directed.

PROBLEMS

1. Why does the ETS make use of different test forms at different administrations of a test? What are the problems this practice causes?

2. In "equating" the scores on two different forms of a given test, how do the test constructions overcome the problem that each of the two forms is used by a *different* group of students?

3. Sam Johnson has received a scaled score of 600 on the verbal section of the SAT. Is this a good score? Explain your answer.

4. In applying the procedure used in "equating" forms the author says: "Here special care must be taken to avoid differential contextual effects." What does he mean by "differential contextual effects"?

5. Susan Smith just took the SAT's and found them surprisingly easy. She is certain that her raw score will be relatively high. Can you make a prediction about her scaled score? Why or why not?

6. In order to allow what it considers fair comparisons of groups of students who take different achievement tests, ETS scales achievement test scores against the expected scores of the entire body of SAT-takers. Explain the scaling procedure employed. In what sense does the procedure seem fair? In what sense does it seem unfair?

7. Consider Figure 1.
    (a) Estimate the most frequently achieved hypothetical score on the physics test for all candidates in the SAT standardization group.
    (b) Estimate the most frequently achieved score of those actually taking the physics test.

8. The author claims the student can't "beat the game" by making strategic choices about which achievement tests to take. Do you agree? Explain your answer. (Hint: Refer to Figure 1.)

9. The physics achievement test has been characterized as one which is taken by a "more able" group of students. Let us say that the subject A achievement test is usually taken by a "less able" group of students. Is it possible to get an 800 on both tests?

10. Notice the scaling procedure of question 6 allows an able student of physics (taken by relatively high SAT students) a higher scaled score than an equally able student of subject A (taken by relatively low SAT students). Explain how ETS "corrects" for this inequity.

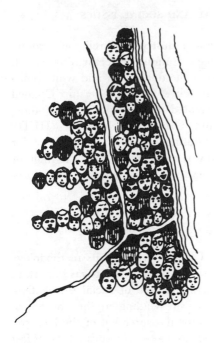

MEASURING RACIAL INTEGRATION POTENTIALS

Brian J. L. Berry   *University of Chicago*

DURING THE summer of 1966, Chicago's racial problems exploded in headlines across the country. The Rev. Dr. Martin Luther King, together with the Chicago Freedom Movement, initiated a series of marches and demonstrations in and around Chicago to highlight the problems of racial segregation in housing. At a rally held in Soldier Field, Dr. King said, "for our primary target we have chosen housing . . . we shall cease to become accomplices to a housing system of discrimination, segregation and degradation. We shall begin to act as if Chicago were an open city."

Reflecting the general conditions of racial unrest, rioting broke out on the west side in July, and National Guardsmen were called out to restore order. Violence and hostility continued throughout the summer, and in this unsettled context a series of meetings took place between the leaders of business, labor, government, civil rights, housing, industry, and religious groups. On December 6, 1966, they signed the Chicago "Summit Agreement" in which they accepted the responsibility for eliminating the dual black and white housing markets that they agreed existed in the city. The Leadership Council for Metropolitan Open Communities was created to carry out this mandate, and the U.S. Department of Housing and Urban Development (HUD) provided the funds to establish the fair housing service. The Center for Urban Studies of The University of Chicago was requested by HUD to monitor the Leadership Council's programs and to evaluate whether they were progressing towards the integration goal.

THE EVALUATION SCHEME

Several problems arose immediately, as the Center developed its methodology and work program. To perform the evaluation task properly it was important to have baseline information about the existing degree of racial segregation, to be able to forecast where existing trends were leading in the absence of the Leadership Council's programs, to have some measurement of the long-run ideal of truly integrated neighborhoods and to have estimates of how fast the ideal might be achieved if every change in residence occurring naturally within the metropolitan area were made so as to contribute to the ideal. Such "baseline" and "maximally-achievable ideal" forecasts were clearly essential if the evaluators were to be able to determine the size of the problem and then to assess whether the Leadership Council's programs were, first, making a difference in the sense that actual events were deviating from the baseline of existing trends and, second, were moving in the direction of the integration goal.

RESEARCH NEEDED

Each of the ingredients presented its own complexities. What, for example, was the degree of racial segregation of Chicago's neighborhoods in 1967, when the Leadership Council began its activities? The last federal census had been taken in 1960, and much change had taken place since that date. What changes might be expected in the spatial distribution of Chicago's black population if present trends and conditions continued? Census information is only available decennially, but we needed to know how changes unfolded on a weekly and monthly basis. Much time and effort had to be devoted to obtaining new kinds of information that permitted continuous monitoring of residential shifts in the Chicago housing market and updating of information on residential segregation. Equally complex was the problem of determining what the racial mixture of neighborhoods would be like in the ideal case, if all real estate transactions were completed in a colorblind housing market, one in which race did not affect the decisions of buyers, tenants, real estate dealers, sellers, or landlords.

MEASURING POTENTIALS

The immediate reaction was to think that this utopian state would exist when the black-white ratio in each neighborhood was the same as in the metropolitan area as a whole. A moment's reflection should indicate that such a uniform ratio is unreasonable, however. For a variety of historical reasons, educational levels and types of job training of blacks and whites now differ, and these differences will persist for many years to come, all the nation's efforts to the contrary notwithstanding. This inertia carries through into the job market, and gives rise to a higher proportion of blacks than whites in lower income categories. In consequence, more blacks than whites have to rent homes, and only a relatively small proportion of black families are able to afford to buy more expensive residences. Proportionately more black purchasers of middle-class homes have two wage-earners rather than one. Black families in lower income levels tend to be larger than white families, thus requiring larger homes or apartments. Further, a disproportionately large share of the poverty families in the central city is black, with female heads of large households looking to public welfare for support.

Somehow, any "ideal" that the evaluators developed had to be well grounded in such facts, recognizing the effects of inertia on existing differences between black and white homeseekers (as well as the fact that the neighborhoods of the city varied considerably in the kinds of housing they had to offer) on the potentials for integration in the next decades. The need to develop some insights into what might be achievable was also important because some observers, for example certain members of the real estate industry, had said that the residential segregation of black and white was the result of a system that takes exactly these differences in income and family type into account, and that there was little distinction, then, between actual conditions and what, ideally, might be achieved. Others, for example, the Leadership Council, argued that even if both income and family differences and the preferences of many families, both black and white, to live in racially homogeneous neighborhoods were taken into account, there was still much scope for increasing integration. The construction by the evaluators of an ideal map representing colorblind mixing subject to the effects of income, family, and other differences could, then, not only quantify the goal toward which the Leadership Council was striving; it could also help resolve the argument about the extent of change the Council might hope to achieve by determining the differences between actual and ideal.

The actual model developed was quite complex, taking many variables into account. A simple example using only one variable, housing expenditures, will serve to illustrate how the evaluators approached this task of measuring racial integration potentials. First, a table was prepared for each census tract in the metropolitan area, listing the number of homes available in each of a series of price and rental classes. The proportion of the families demanding homes in each of these classes in the metropolitan area as a whole who were black was also calculated. It was assumed that this proportion could be used as a measure of the probability that a homeseeker coming to the tract looking for a home in this category would be black if the housing market and individual homeseekers were completely indifferent to color. Thus, if there were 50,000 families demanding homes of category A in the metropolitan area and 20,000 were black, the probability that a family selected at random from the 50,000 would be black is $20,000/50,000 = 0.4$. If tract 1 has 1000 homes in category A, the expected number of black occupants is therefore $1000 \times 0.4 = 400$ on the average in the colorblind market, although there clearly could be random variations from this. Similarly, if the metropolitan probability of a black family demanding a home in price range B, is 0.2 and there are 750 homes of this range in tract 1, the expected number of black occupants is $0.2 \times 750 = 150$. The several expectations can be summed $(400 + 150 + . . .)$, to yield the predicted number of black families in tract 1. This, divided by the total number of homes in the tract, gives the expected black percentage, which usually differed from the actual black percentage currently observable in the tract. The difference in percentages is called the percentage redistributive shift required if present segregation is to be changed to the ideal of integration.

The various percentages can be mapped to show spatial variations. Figure 1, for example, maps the predicted black percentages computed for every census tract in metropolitan Chicago, using a more complex version of the model described above in which the expenditure categories were subdivided by household size, and each of the resulting categories was in turn subdivided into successively smaller groups on the basis of additional variables, including the sex of the household head. In the map, different shades have been applied to the census tracts to indicate different percentage ranges. The map reveals that few neighborhoods would have more than twenty percent of their residents black in this utopian case. These are largely older central-city neighborhoods in which large apartments are available at low rents in deteriorating buildings, or areas in which there are new clusters of public housing.

Massive shifts in racial patterns would be required to achieve the levels of integration corresponding to the patterns of Figure 1. These are shown in Figure 2, which maps the redistributive percentages—differences between the ideal and today's actual percentages—calculated in the model from which Figure 1 was derived. To move from present racial patterns to the ideal would require, the map shows, 10 to 20% increases in the percentage of

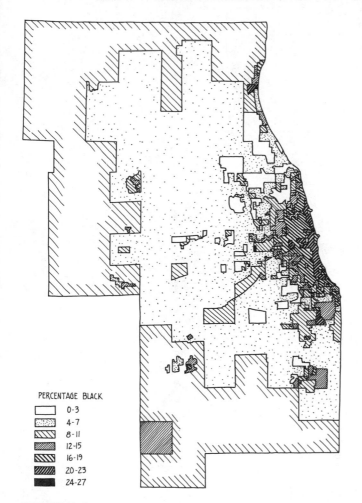

PERCENTAGE BLACK

	0-3
	4-7
	8-11
	12-15
	16-19
	20-23
	24-27

FIGURE 1

*Distribution of the black popu-
lation in a colorblind housing
market with expenditure standardization*

black households in most suburban areas and decreases of more than 60%
in the existing central city ghetto neighborhoods.

How fast could the ideal of colorblind mixing be achieved under natural
moving rates? Analyses of residential mobility indicated that a minimum
of seven to eight years would be required if all relocations of families nor-
mally occurring within the metropolitan area, as they change residences to
adjust them to changing needs and income levels, were made so as to integrate

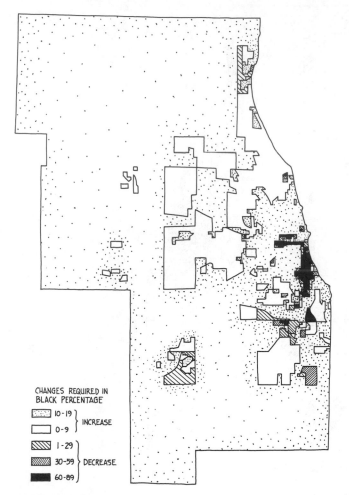

CHANGES REQUIRED IN
BLACK PERCENTAGE

10 - 19 } INCREASE
0 - 9   }

1 - 29   }
30 - 59 } DECREASE
60 - 89 }

FIGURE 2

*Redistribution of the black
population to achieve expen-
diture-standardized equality*

neighborhoods now segregated.   Of course, this is the lower limit of the time
required under the most favorable circumstances.   In so far as families'
changes of residence, made as they are to increase satisfactions with home
and neighborhood, are inconsistent with increasing integration (as, for example, when a white resident of one of today's integrated communities receives
a promotion and moves to an area in which the black percentage expected
in terms of the model is lower), a much longer time will be needed.   On the
other hand, to the extent that both black and white prefer to live in racially

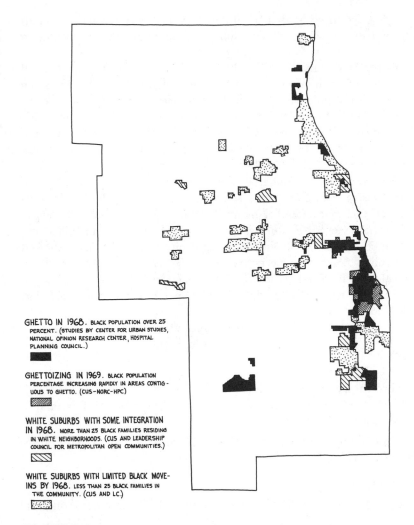

GHETTO IN 1968. BLACK POPULATION OVER 25 PERCENT. (STUDIES BY CENTER FOR URBAN STUDIES, NATIONAL OPINION RESEARCH CENTER, HOSPITAL PLANNING COUNCIL.)

GHETTOIZING IN 1969. BLACK POPULATION PERCENTAGE INCREASING RAPIDLY IN AREAS CONTIG- UOUS TO GHETTO. (CUS-NORC-HPC)

WHITE SUBURBS WITH SOME INTEGRATION IN 1968. MORE THAN 25 BLACK FAMILIES RESIDING IN WHITE NEIGHBORHOODS. (CUS AND LEADERSHIP COUNCIL FOR METROPOLITAN OPEN COMMUNITIES.)

WHITE SUBURBS WITH LIMITED BLACK MOVE- INS BY 1968. LESS THAN 25 BLACK FAMILIES IN THE COMMUNITY. (CUS AND LC.)

FIGURE 3
Racial makeup and trends in metropolitan Chicago

homogeneous neighborhoods, Figure 2 may overstate the degree of integration desired.

THE EVALUATION

The primary goal in the Center's efforts was to provide a framework for evaluating the Leadership Council's programs by providing baseline data and measuring the goals that the Council aspired to achieve. This evaluation was still in progress as of mid-1970 although a first-year evaluation report entitled *Down from the Summit* was submitted to HUD by the Center in late 1969.

When this report was made, only a little progress in suburban areas could be reported, and in fact the central-city ghetto was characterized by increasing rather than decreasing polarization. Real estate agents' dual listings, the racial fears and prejudices of whites fleeing to suburbia, and the increasing feeling among blacks that integration is undesirable limited most additional housing available to blacks to neighborhoods contiguous to the existing ghetto. This in turn resulted in a wavelike pattern of ghetto expansion.

As for the Leadership Council, it could report that some suburbs had enacted fair housing ordinances and some now had a few black residents (Figure 3). Of 902 black families living in otherwise white suburban neighborhoods, 544 had moved in during the years 1967–68. Meanwhile, very few white families moved back into the central city where our maps showed that countervailing flows were necessary, except where public investment in urban renewal was involved. Clearly, massive efforts will be necessary in the future if society truly believes that integration is an important goal that must be achieved.

PROBLEMS

1. What were the types of information the Urban Studies Center felt it needed before it could begin to evaluate the success of the Leadership Council's integration program?

2. What is meant by "maximally-achievable ideal forecast"? How does it enter into the evaluation process?

Consider the table:

Home Category		Metropolitan Demand (families)		Number of Homes in
		Total	Black	Selected Census Tract
$10,000	$20,000	200,000	100,000	100
$20,000	$40,000	400,000	150,000	300
$40,000	$60,000	200,000	50,000	500
$60,000	$80,000	100,000	20,000	200
$80,000	$100,000	50,000	10,000	100

Using the technique outlined by the author, answer questions 3 through 5.

3. How many black-owned homes in the $40,000–$60,000 range would you expect in the selected tract with a colorblind market?

4. What *percentage* of the homes in the $20,000–$40,000 range would you expect to be *white-owned* in the selected tract with a colorblind market?

5. What would be the total expected number of black-owned homes in the selected tract with a colorblind market?

6. Suppose the total black population of Chicago is 30%. According to Figure 1, most of the northern quarter of Chicago would have 4–11% black residents in a colorblind market. Explain this concept of integration.

7. (a) If there were no racial or other biases at work in the housing market, what relationship would you expect between the racial percentage in a given neighborhood and in the city as a whole? Explain.

(b) What does the author call the situation in which only economic biases exist?

8. Refer to Figure 2. Estimate the percentage of the city's area which would require an increase in its black population to achieve integration.

9. Suppose a census tract had the following composition:

	No. of units available	% white Chicago families seeking housing in this category
Housing category A	500	50
Housing category B	300	90
Housing category C	200	60

What percentage of this census tract would be white, assuming a colorblind housing market? How would the study characterize this census tract? (Hint: Refer to Figure 3.)

10. Notice the author intimates that *current* residential mobility rates were used in estimating how long it would take to achieve the "ideal" integrated arrangements. If total or even partial success were achieved in the establishment of a colorblind market though, would you expect *current* overall mobility rates, for blacks at least, to go up or down? Why?

11. Describe the overall results of the Urban Studies Center evaluation of the Leadership Council's program. Might the success (or lack of success) found have to do with other factors besides the activities of the Leadership Council? If you say "no", why not? If you say "yes", name a few such factors.

MEASURING THE EFFECTS OF SOCIAL INNOVATIONS BY MEANS OF TIME SERIES*

Donald T. Campbell   *Northwestern University*

WE LIVE in an age of social reforms, of large-scale efforts to correct specific social problems. In the past most such efforts have not been adequately evaluated: usually there has been no scientifically valid evidence as to whether the problem was alleviated or not. Since there are always a variety of proposed solutions for any one problem, as well as numerous other problems calling for funds and attention, it becomes important that society be able to learn how effective any specific innovation has been.

From the statistician's point of view, the best designed experiments, whether in the laboratory or out in the community, involve setting up an *experimental group* and a *control group* similar in every way possible to the experimental

* Supported in part by NSF grant GS 1309X.

group except that it does not receive the same experimental treatment.   The statistician's way of achieving this all-purpose equivalence of experimental and control groups is randomization.   Persons (or plots of land or other units) are assigned at random (as by the roll of dice) to either an experimental or a control group.   After the treatment, the two groups are compared, and the differences that are larger than chance would explain are attributed to the experimental treatment.   This ideal procedure is beginning to be used in pilot tests of social policy, as in the current New Jersey negative income-tax experiment where several hundred low income employed families who agreed to cooperate have been randomly assigned to experimental groups that receive income supplements of differing sizes and a control group that receives no financial aid.   The effects of this aid on the amounts of other earnings, on health, family stability, and the like are being studied.

While such experimental designs are ideal, they are not often feasible. They are impossible to use, for example, in evaluating any new program which is applied to all citizens at once, as most legal changes are.   In these more common situations much less satisfactory modes of experimental inference must suffice.   The *interrupted time series design,* on which this paper will concentrate, is one of the most useful of these quasi-experimental designs. The proper interpretation of such data presents complex statistical problems, some of which are not yet adequately solved.   This paper will touch upon a number of these, in terms of words and graphs rather than mathematical symbols.   The discussion will start off by considering two actual cases.

THE CONNECTICUT CRACKDOWN ON SPEEDING

On December 23, 1955, Connecticut instituted an exceptionally severe and prolonged crackdown on speeding.   Like most public reporting of program effectiveness, the results were reported in terms of simple before-and-after measures: a comparison of this year's figures with those of a year ago.   The 1956 total of 284 traffic deaths was compared with the 1955 total of 324, and the governor stated, "With a saving of 40 lives in 1956 . . . we can say the program is definitely worthwhile."   Figure 1 presents his data graphically.   This simple quasi-experimental design is very weak and deceptive. There are so many other possible explanations for the change from 324 to 284 highway fatalities.   In attributing all of this change to his crackdown, the governor is making the implicit assumption that without the crackdown there would have been no change at all.   A time series presentation, using the fatality records of several prior and subsequent years, adds greatly to the strength of the analysis.   Figure 2 shows such data for the Connecticut crackdown.   In this larger context the 1955–56 drop looks trivial.   We can see that the implicit assumption underlying the governor's statement was almost certainly wrong.

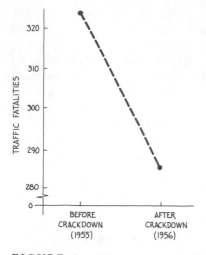

FIGURE 1

Connecticut traffic fatalities, 1955–56. Source: Campbell and Ross (1968)

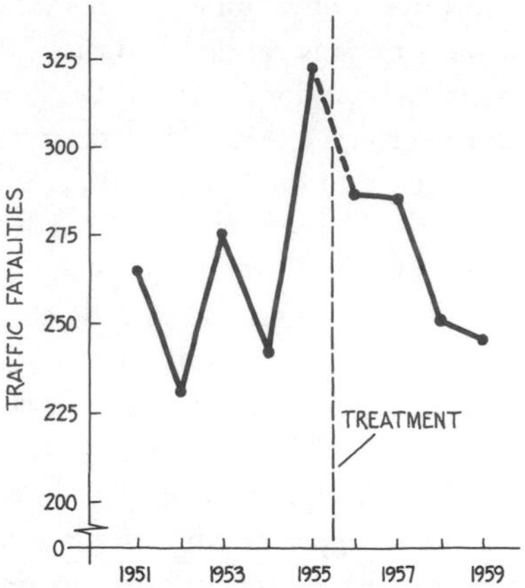

FIGURE 2

Connecticut traffic fatalities, 1951–59. Source: Campbell and Ross (1968)

To explore this more fully, turn to Figure 3, which presents in a stylized manner how an identical shift in values before and after a treatment can in some instances be clearcut evidence of an effect, and in other cases no evidence at all of a change. Thus with only 1955 and 1956 data to go on, that drop of 40 traffic fatalities shown in Figure 1 might have been a part of a steady annual drop already in progress (the reverse of the steady rise in line F of Figure 3), or of an unstable zigzag (as in line G of Figure 3), etc. Figure 2 shows that in Connecticut, the unstable zigzag is the case. The 1955–56 drop is about the same size as the drops of 1951–52, 1953–54, and 1957–58, times when no crackdowns were present to explain them. Furthermore, the 1955–56 drop is only half the size of the 1954–55 rise. Thus with all this previous instability in full graphic view, one would be unlikely to claim all of any year-to-year change as due to a crackdown, as the governor seemed to do.

Later, we shall examine Figure 2 again to raise a more difficult problem of inference. But before we do this, let's spend more time on the stability issue, with the help of an illustration from a reform that even a skeptical methodologist can believe was successful.

THE BRITISH "BREATHALYSER" CRACKDOWN OF 1967

In September 1967, the British government started a new program of enforcement with regard to drunken driving. It took its popular name from a device for ascertaining the degree of intoxication from a sample of a person's breath.

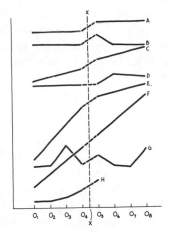

FIGURE 3

Some possible outcome patterns from the introduction of a treatment at point X into a time series of measurements, O_1 to O_8. The $O_4 - O_5$ gain is the same for all time series, except for D, while the legitimacy of inferring an effect varies widely, being strongest in A and B, and totally unjustified in F, G, and H. Source: Campbell and Stanley (1963)

Police administered this simple test to drivers stopped on suspicion, and if it showed intoxication, then took them into the police station for more thorough tests. This new testing procedure was accompanied by more stringent punishment, including suspension of license. Figure 4 shows the effect of this crackdown on Friday and Saturday night casualties (fatalities plus serious injuries). The effect is dramatically clear. There is an immediate drop of around 40% and a leveling off at a level that seems some 30% below the precrackdown rate, although this is hard to tell for sure since we don't know what changes time would have brought in the casualty rate without the crackdown.

Does the effect show up when casualties at all hours of all days are totaled? Figure 5 shows such data. While the effect is probably still there, it is cer-

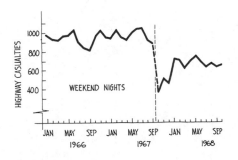

FIGURE 4

Effects of the September 1967 English "Breathalyser" crackdown on drunken driving. Fatalities plus serious injuries, Fridays and Saturdays, 10:00 PM to 4:00 AM, by month. Source: Ross et al. (1970)

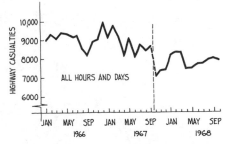

FIGURE 5

Effects of the September 1967 English "Breathalyser" crackdown. Fatalities plus serious injuries, all hours and days, by month. Source: Ross et al. (1970)

tainly less clear, the crackdown drop being not much larger than the unexplained instability of other time periods. (The crackdown drop is, however, the largest month-to-month change, not only during the plotted period, but also for a longer period going back to 1961, for these data from which the seasonal fluctuations have been removed.)

THE STATISTICAL ANALYSIS OF INSTABILITY

The problem of the statistician is to formalize the grounds for inference that we have used informally or intuitively in our judgments from these graphs. It is clear that the more unstable the line is before the policy change or treatment point, the bigger the difference has to be to impress us as a real effect. One approach of statisticians is to assume that the time series is a result of a general trend plus specific random deviations at each time period. The theory of this type of analysis is well worked out for the case in which the random deviations at each point are completely independent of deviations at other points. But in real-life situations the sources of deviation or perturbation at any one point are apt to be similar for adjacent and near points in time, and dissimilar for more remote points. This creates deceptive situations both for statistical tests of significance and for visual interpretation. Figures 6 and 7 illustrate this with computer simulated time series. For each point in time, times 1 to 40, there is a *true score*. These true scores, if plotted,

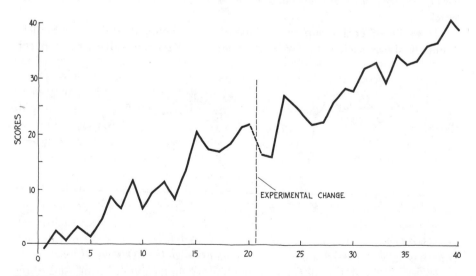

FIGURE 6

Simulated time series with in-dependent error. Source: Ross et al. (1970)

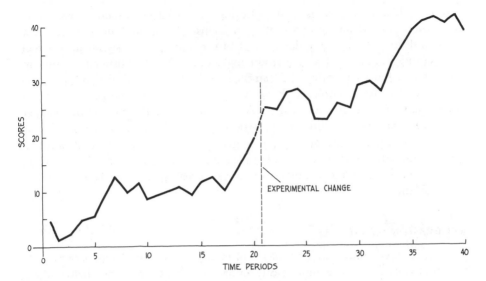

FIGURE 7
Simulated time series with correlated (lagged) error. Source: Campbell (1969)

would make a straight diagonal line from a lower left score of zero to an upper right score of 40, with no bump whatsoever at the hypothetical treatment point. These true scores are the same for Figures 6 and 7. To each true score has been added or subtracted a randomly chosen deviation. In Figure 6, the deviation at each time point was drawn independently of every other deviation. This is a simulation of the case in which the hypothetical treatment introduced between time periods 20 and 21 had no effect at all. Occasionally, by chance, random deviations will occur in such a pattern so as to make it look as though the treatment had an effect, as perhaps in Figure 6. It is the task of *tests of significance* to estimate when the difference from before treatment to after treatment is more than such random deviations could account for. Statistical formulas have been worked out which do this well in the case of independent deviations such as Figure 6 illustrates.

Figure 7 is based upon the same straight diagonal line as Figure 6. It has the same magnitude of deviations added. But the deviations are no longer independent. Instead, four smaller deviations have been added at each point, in a staggered or lagged pattern. A new deviation is introduced at each time period and persists for three subsequent periods. As a result, each point shares three such deviations with the period immediately prior and three with the period immediately following. It shares two deviations with periods 2 steps away in either direction, and one deviation with periods 3 steps away. For periods 4 or more steps away, the deviations are independent. While

Figure 7, like Figure 6, is a straight line distorted by random error, note how much more dynamic and cyclical it seems. Such nonindependent deviations mislead both visual judgments of effect and tests of significance which assume independence, through producing judgments of statistically significant effect much too frequently. (To emphasize the lack of any true or systematic departures, let it be emphasized that were one to repeat each simulation 1000 times, and to average the results, each average would approximate the perfectly straight diagonal line of the true scores.) There is a variety of ways in which statisticians are attempting to get appropriate tests of significance for the real-life situations in which nonindependent deviations are characteristic. While none is completely satisfactory as yet, great strides are being made on the problem.

REGRESSION ARTIFACTS

We have moved from simple problems of inference to more complex ones. We will return soon to some more easily understood problems. But before doing that, let us attempt to understand a final difficult problem, known in one statistical tradition as *regression artifacts*. If we can be sure that the policy change took place independently of the ups and downs of the previous time periods, there is no worry. But if the timing of the policy change was chosen just because of an extreme value immediately prior, then a "regression artifact" will be sufficient to explain the occurrence of subsequent less extreme values. To see if a regression artifact might be at work in the Connecticut case, let us return to Figure 2. Here we can note that the most dramatic change in the whole series is the 1954–55 increase. By studying the newspapers and the governor's pronouncements, we can tell that it was this striking increase which caused him to initiate the crackdown. Thus the treatment came when it did because of the 1955 high point.

In any unstable time series, after any point which is an extreme departure from the general trend, the subsequent points will on the average be nearer the general trend. Try this out on Figure 6. Move your eye from left to right, noting each point that is "the highest so far." For most of these, the next point is lower, or has *regressed* toward the general trend. Such regression subsequent to points selected for their extremity is an automatic feature of the very fact of instability and should not be given a causal interpretation. Applied to Figure 2, this means that even with no true effect from the crackdown at all, we would expect 1956 to be lower than the extreme of 1955.

OTHER REASONS FOR SHIFTS IN TIME SERIES

It is going to be important for administrators, legislators, the voting public, and other groups of nonstatisticians to be able to draw conclusions from time series data on important public programs.   For this reason, two further points will be made that are less directly statistical.   First note that there are many reasons for abrupt shifts in time series other than the introduction of a program change.   One very deceptive reason is a shift in record keeping procedures. Such shifts are apt to be made at the same time as other policy changes.   For example, a major change in Chicago's police system came in 1959 when Professor Orlando Wilson was brought in from the University of California to reform a corrupt police department.   Figure 8 shows his apparent effect on thefts—a dramatic *increase*.   This turns out to be due to his reform of the record keeping system, and the rise was anticipated for that reason.

In a real situation, unlike in an insulated laboratory, many other causes may be operating at the same time as the experimental policy change.   Thus in Connecticut or in England, a drop in traffic casualties might have been due to especially dry weather, or fewer cars on the road, or to new safety devices, or to a multitude of other factors.   If one had been able to design an experiment with the randomized control groups discussed at the beginning of this essay, such explanations would have been ruled out statistically.   However, setting up such an experiment would have been impossible in these two situations.   We must instead try to rule out these rival explanations of an effect in other ways.   One useful approach is to look at newspaper records of rainfall, changes in traffic density, and other possible causes of the shift.

Another approach is to look for some control comparison that should show the effects of these other causes, if they are operating, but where the specific reform treatment was not applied.   For Connecticut, the data from four nearby states are relevant, as shown in Figure 9.   All of these states should have been affected by changes in weather, new safety features in cars, etc. While these data support the notion that the 1955 Connecticut fatalities would

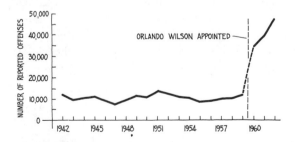

FIGURE 8

Reported larcenies under $50 in Chicago from 1942 to 1962. Source: Campbell   (1969). Data from Uniform Crime Reports for the United States, 1942–62.

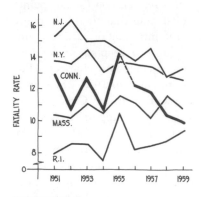

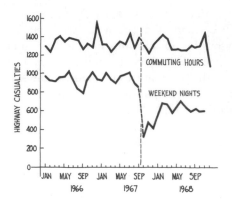

FIGURE 9

Traffic fatalities for Connecticut, New York, New Jersey, Rhode Island, and Massachusetts (per 100,000 persons). Source: Campbell (1969)

FIGURE 10

A comparison of casualties during closed hours (commuting hours) and weekend nights in the English "Breathalyser" crackdown. Source: Ross et al. (1970)

have been lower than 1955 even without the crackdown, the persisting decline throughout 1957, 1958, and 1959 is much the steepest in Connecticut, and may well indicate a genuine effect of the prolonged crackdown. While visually we have little difficulty in using these supplementary data, the statistician has many real problems in combining them all in an appropriate test of significance.

For England, there were no appropriate comparison nations available. But British pubs are closed before and during commuting hours, so casualties from such hours provide a kind of comparison base, as shown in Figure 10. Unfortunately there is a lot of instability in these data so that they do not enable us to estimate with much confidence the degree to which the initial crackdown effects are persisting.

A FINAL NOTE

There are several general lessons to be learned from these brief illustrations. The first involves the distinction between *true experiments,* in which experimental and control groups are assigned by randomization, and *quasi experiments.* True experiments, when they are possible, offer much greater power and precision of inference than do quasi experiments. The administrators of social innovations, in consultation with statisticians, should attempt to use such designs where possible. Where true experiments are not possible, or have not been used, there are some quasi-experimental designs such as the interrupted time series which can be very useful in evaluating policy changes. These too require statistical skill to avoid misleading conclusions. Evaluation of social innovations is an important and challenging area of application for modern statistics.

PROBLEMS

1. Why is the design on which the paper concentrates called an *interrupted* time series design?

2. How does Figure 2 change your perception of Figure 1?

3. Consider Figure 3. Suppose that X was a currency devaluation which resulted in a price increase between 0_4 and 0_5. What effect did X have on the price of product F? Product A? Product C?

4. Consider Figure 3. Why does the author say that one can most legitimately infer an effect in A and B while totally unjustified in inferring one in F, G, and H?

5. Consider Figures 4 and 5. Is the effect of the breathalyser crackdown more pronounced in one of the figures? If so, which one?

6. (a) Explain the difference between independent and lagged error.
   (b) How would you characterize the effects of the two types of error on the plots of data in Figures 6 and 7?

7. What does the author mean when he says Figure 7 is more "dynamic and cyclical" than Figure 6?

8. Explain what the author means by the term *regression artifact*.

9. Refer to Figure 8. Explain the sharp increase in the number of reported offenses when Orlando Wilson was appointed.

10. Should the 1955–56 traffic fatality decline in Rhode Island (Figure 9) be attributed to the speeding crackdown in neighboring Connecticut? Explain your answer.

11. What is a *true experiment*? What is a *quasi-experiment*?

12. Comment on this statement: Quasi-experiments are used in evaluating policy changes because it is virtually impossible to apply true experimental design to social situations.

REFERENCES

D. T. Campbell. 1969. "Reforms as Experiments." *American Psychologist* 24:4, pp. 409–429.

D. T. Campbell and H. L. Ross. 1968. "The Connecticut Crackdown on Speeding: Time-Series Data in Quasi-Experimental Analysis." *Law & Society Review* 3:1, pp. 33–53.

D. T. Campbell and J. C. Stanley. 1963. "Experimental and Quasi-Experimental Designs for Research on Teaching." N. L. Gage, ed., *Handbook of Research on Teaching*. Chicago: Rand-McNally. Pp. 171–246. Reprinted as *Experimental and Quasi-Experimental Designs for Research*. 1966. Chicago: Rand-McNally.

H. L. Ross, D. T. Campbell, and G. V. Glass. 1970. "Determining the Social Effects of a Legal Reform: The British 'Breathalyser' Crackdown of 1967." *American Behavioral Scientist* 15:1, pp. 110–113.

J. S. Wholey, J. W. Scanlon, H. G. Duffy, J. S. Fukamato, and L. M. Vogt. 1970. *Federal Evaluation Policy*. 9-121-21. Washington: The Urban Institute.

OPINION POLLING IN A DEMOCRACY

George Gallup *Chairman, American Institute of Public Opinion*

IN ONE form or another, the public opinion poll has been part of the American scene for well over 100 years. As early as July 24, 1824, a report in the Harrisburg *Pennsylvania* told of a "straw vote taken without discrimination of parties" which indicated Jackson to be the popular presidential choice over Adams. Polls of a more careful nature than "straws" were occasionally undertaken in the early part of the current century, but these did not generally deal with issues of the day. It was not until the mid-thirties that polls based on carefully drawn samples were undertaken on a continuing basis.

The superiority of polls based on scientific sampling procedures over those which relied for their validity only on the size of an unscientifically chosen group of persons was demonstrated in dramatic fashion by the 1936 presidential election when Franklin D. Roosevelt defeated Alfred E. Landon in a landslide vote. A Landon victory had been predicted by the *Literary Digest*, a magazine which ran the oldest, largest, and most widely publicized of the polls at that time.   The *Digest*'s final prediction was based on 2,376,523 questionnaires by mail. Yet despite the massive size of this sample, it failed to predict a Roosevelt victory, being off the mark by 19 percentage points.   The Gallup Poll and the Roper Poll, on the other hand, predicted a Roosevelt victory.

The failure of the *Literary Digest*'s polling approach can be explained rather simply. The *Digest*'s sample of voters was drawn from lists of automobile and telephone owners.   This sampling system produced accurate results so long as voters in average and above-average income groups were as likely to vote Democratic as Republican; and conversely those in the lower income brackets— the have-nots—were as likely to vote for either party candidate.   With the advent of the New Deal, however, the American electorate became sharply stratified along income lines, with many persons in the above-average income groups gravitating to the Republican party and many of those in the below-average income groups moving to the Democratic side.

Obviously, a sampling system that reached only telephone subscribers and automobile owners—who were largely among the better-off in that era—was certain to overestimate Republican strength in the 1936 election.   And that is precisely what did happen.

In contrast, the scientific sampling methods which were employed by Gallup, Elmo Roper, and Archibald Crossley for the first time in this election were designed to include the proper proportion of voters from each economic stratus—not just those who owned automobiles and telephones.   These samples much more accurately reflected the proportion of Democrats and Republicans in the population.   And the findings produced by the three organizations, therefore, were closer to the actual election results.

The 1936 election experience provides an excellent example of how election polling serves the science of opinion measurement by providing a kind of "acid test" of statistical methods.   An election represents one of the few situations in which the figures produced by survey organizations can be compared to the actual voting results.

The progress made in polling techniques since 1935 is revealed by examining the error between the Gallup Poll's final election figures and the actual vote. For the seven national elections between 1936 and 1948, the average error recorded for the Gallup Poll was 4.0 percentage points.   For the 11 national elections since 1948, the average error is 1.6 points.

The Gallup Poll and other survey organizations have demonstrated that when scientific methods, rather than procedures relying heavily on subjective judgment, are employed, the prediction of aggregate human behavior can be closely approximated.

The American Institute of Public Opinion was founded in the fall of 1935 for the purpose of determining the public's views on the important political, social, and economic issues of the day.   The operation, as planned, was to be continuous, with survey reports prepared for distribution at regular intervals. The press and the press services traditionally had confined their efforts largely to reporting events—*what people do.* This new effort was designed to deal with a different aspect of life—*what people think.*

The need for a way to measure public opinion had been suggested near the end of the last century by James Bryce, an Englishman who had established himself as a leading authority on the American government. In his book *The American Commonwealth,* which was widely used in American universities, Bryce observed, "The obvious weakness of government by public opinion is the difficulty of ascertaining it." He predicted that the next and final stage in the development of democracies would be reached when the will of the people could be known at all times.

This final stage as predicted by Bryce is close at hand. With developments of recent years, it is now possible to poll a sample of the entire U.S. in a matter of hours. In fact, there is little difference today in the speed with which the media of communications cover major events and the speed with which opinions can be gathered regarding these same events. National surveys have been conducted in a matter of hours to measure first reactions to occurrences such as the nationwide postal strike in 1970 and the Calley verdict in 1971. Also, Gallup affiliates in countries around the world have frequently measured multinational opinion in as little time as 72 hours about such events as the launching of the first Sputnik in 1957 and the visit of Soviet Premier Khrushchev to the U.S. in 1959.

In 1922, Walter Lippmann, in a prophetic statement in his widely read and quoted book *Public Opinion* said "The social scientist will acquire his dignity and his strength when he has worked out his method. He will do that by turning into opportunity the need of the great society for *instruments of analysis* by which an invisible and most stupendously difficult environment can be made intelligible."

The environment has not become any less complex in the half century since Lippmann wrote these words. And the modern poll is at least one instrument of analysis that can and does help to make the environment more intelligible.

DETERMINING AREAS OF IGNORANCE

Some critics have questioned the value of opinion polling, saying that the great mass of people are uninformed on most issues of the day, and therefore, their views have little significance. If persons in a survey feel that they are not competent to answer certain questions or have no opinion because they lack information, they will usually say they don't know or have no opinion. Moreover, opinions that have most significance concern issues or problems that touch the daily lives of the general public. And the range of these is great; in fact, it covers most of the vital issues of the day.

On some issues, it is important to separate informed opinion from the uninformed. This can be accomplished by a simple survey procedure devised by the Gallup Poll. It is a series of questions that begins: "Have you heard or read about X issue?" The respondent can answer either "yes" or "no." If the answer is "yes," the respondent is asked "Please tell me in your own words what you consider the chief issue to be." And the interviewer writes the respondent's exact words on his interviewing form. The next question seeks to discover the extent, or level, of the respondent's knowledge of the subject. The respondent may be asked to state the positions held by various people or countries involved in a controversy, for example. The next question asks "How do you think this issue should be resolved?" or, depending on the nature of the controversy, a variation of this question. The respondent is permitted to explain his views with as many qualifications as he wishes.

The next in the series poses specific questions that can be answered "yes" or "no." Often it is possible to explain the issue in a few sentences (in effect, to inform the person being interviewed) and then to record his opinions. Individuals who say they have not heard or read about the issue are eligible at this point to answer both this and the last question.

The last question is intended to establish the "intensity" with which the respondent holds his views. How strongly does he feel that he is right? What steps would he be willing to take to implement his opinions?

Thus we have seen that not all questions asked in a public opinion poll are of the yes-no variety. Complex problems, as pointed out, typically require a series of questions. But eventually all issues, especially those dealt with by legislative bodies, sooner or later have to be resolved and the legislator must, whether he likes it or not, vote "yes" or "no." In similar fashion, the ordinary voter, whether he is voting on candidates in a presidential election or on a state referendum issue, must eventually cast a simple "yes" or "no" vote. There is no provision on the ballot or voting machine for qualifications or modifications. He can't put his X in a box marked "no opinion," though, of course, he can skip voting on the issue.

In the process of discovering what the public knows in certain areas, it is possible to shed light on the strengths and weaknesses of the educational system which has brought the public to its present level of knowledge. The best way to judge the quality of the product, and one of the key functions of a polling operation, is to determine levels of knowledge and "areas of ignorance."

The survey approach to social problems has been widely accepted. As Professor Kenneth Boulding has written

> Perhaps the most important single development pointing towards more scientific images of social systems is the improvement in the collection and processing of social information. The method of sample surveys is the telescope of the social sciences. It enables us to scan the social universe, at some small cost in statistical error, in ways we have never been able to do before.

SOME EXAMPLES OF SURVEY RESULTS

Since 1935, the Gallup Poll has published over 6500 reports covering a wide range of subjects. Following are some of the questions asked in recent months and the national findings.

What is the SMALLEST amount of money a family of four (husband, wife, and two children) needs each week to get along in this community? (Reported: Jan. 7, 1972)

Median of responses (Nonfarm families) : $127 per week

If you had to register again today—or if you are now under 21 and would be registering for the first time—would you register as a Democrat or as a Republican? (Based on projections of the total number of citizens of voting age in the United States—excluding institutionalized persons.) (Reported: November 28, 1971)

68,000,000. . . . . Democrats
38,000,000. . . . . Republicans
25,000,000. . . . . Undecided

If your party nominated a woman for President, would you vote for her if she were qualified for the job? (Reported: August 5, 1971)

Yes. 66%
No. 29%
No opinion. 5%

Let us look briefly at some other issues and what the public has to say about them. (Of course the wording of questions makes a difference in how people answer, but the following will serve to give some idea of public sentiment as determined by the Gallup Poll.)

A majority of Americans would like to overhaul the whole process of electing a president; they favor nationwide primaries, making the conventions, if held, more dignified, shortening the campaign, and abandoning the present electoral college system. Long before such legislation was passed, polls showed that our fellow citizens wanted the voting age lowered to 18. Americans favor stiffer laws on drinking and driving, tougher gun laws, less leniency toward criminals on the part of courts, compulsory arbitration in the case of strikes (particularly those strikes affecting the public welfare), tougher laws on pornography, guaranteed work rather than a guaranteed annual income. Americans think all young men should be required to give one year's service to their country, either in the armed forces or in some nonmilitary work, such as VISTA or the Peace Corps.

OTHER CONTRIBUTIONS OF SAMPLE SURVEYS

Even more important are the contributions that sample surveys of the population can make in the improvement of government. The modern poll can, and to a certain extent does, function as a *creative arm of government*. It can discover the likely response of the public to any new proposal, law, or innovation. It can do this by presenting ideas to the public for their appraisal and judgment—ideas that range from specific proposals for dealing with strikes and racial problems to proposals for ending the war in Vietnam.

More and more, the modern poll is dealing with new ideas or proposals for dealing in new ways with current problems. The poll in this respect has a natural advantage over legislators. It can go directly to the people without fear of political repercussions. It can determine the degree of acceptance of or resistance to any proposal—its appeal or lack of appeal, at least in its early stages of acceptance or rejection. It is this creative function that may, in the years ahead, offer the public opinion poll its greatest opportunity for service to the nation.

In many ways it is unfortunate that modern polls should be closely identified in the minds of so many persons with elections and election predictions. Although election polling is an important part of the work of survey organizations, providing important evidence of the accuracy of polling methods and of progress in the technology of this field, the prominence given election polling frequently tends to obscure the many other functions that modern polls can perform to make the political environment more intelligible. In fact, polls can do things that were scarcely dreamed of in earlier days. For example, the modern poll can simulate a national election by determining the relative strength of candidates, pitting leading contenders against each other, in any combination. It can also simulate a nationwide referendum on any issue of current importance. And the results arrived at through polling can be expected to differ little from a national election or referendum held at the same time.

The modern poll can provide a continuous check on the popularity of the president—a sort of American equivalent of a vote of confidence in the government such as that found in those nations with a parliamentary form of government. The Gallup Poll's measurement of presidential popularity has been used at regular intervals during the administrations of six presidents. It has proved to be a sensitive barometer of public attitudes regarding the president, with wide fluctuations recorded in approval and disapproval.

For example, President Nixon's highest approval rating to date, 68%, was recorded in a survey conducted following his nationwide televised speech in November 1969, in which he spelled out his program for Vietnamization of the war. The President's low point, 48% approval, was recorded in June 1971, a time when the state of the economy undoubtedly was an important factor. President Johnson's high point, 80%, was registered soon after he took office in November 1963, following the death of President Kennedy. His low point, 35% approval, came in August 1968, when Gallup surveys showed disillusionment over our involvement in Vietnam at a peak.

The modern poll can beam a bright and devastating light on the gap which too often exists between the will of the people and the translation of this will into law by legislators. From years of measuring how the average citizen reacts to a wide range of ideas, it is clear that his thinking is sound, his common-sense quotient high. Congressional action, as a matter of fact, supports this belief; historically, it has been true that sooner or later the public's will is translated into law.

PROBLEMS

1. Describe the *Literary Digest's* sampling system for its 1936 poll. Was this "scientific sampling"? Why or why not? Why was the poll so far off in predicting the election result?

2. Letters to the editor also reflect public opinion. In what ways is polling a better way of soliciting this opinion?

3. What might a pollster mean by "area of ignorance"?

4. Explain the procedure the Gallup Poll uses to separate "informed" and "uninformed" opinion on an issue.

5. Comment on the following statement: The polling process ultimately elicits a simple yes or no from the respondent.

6. What *percentage* of registerable voters were estimated to be Democrats in November 1971?

7. In the poll on party affiliation, does an answer of "undecided" mean that the respondent can't decide between "Democrat" and "Republican"? What about other parties?

8. (a) The final pre-election poll shows a neck-and-neck race between presidential candidates. What effect would you expect this to have on voter turnout? (See the article by Tufte.)

(b) If the poll showed the following:

Candidate A	55%
Candidate B	35%
Undecided	10%

would you expect the winner prediction to be correct? What level of voter turnout would you expect?

9. How does polling serve as a "creative arm of government"?

REFERENCES

James Bryce. 1888. *The American Commonwealth,* vol. 2. New York: AMS Press.

Walter Lippmann. 1965. *Public Opinion.* New York: Free Press.

HOW WELL DO SOCIAL INNOVATIONS WORK? *

John P. Gilbert   *Harvard University*
Richard J. Light   *Harvard University*
Frederick Mosteller   *Harvard University*

HOW EFFECTIVE are modern large-scale social action programs? To see how well such programs accomplish their primary mission, we have reviewed the performance of a large number. Our examples are drawn from public and private social action programs, from applied social research, and from studies in medicine and mental illness. We have two purposes in mind: first, to find out how frequently social innovations succeed, and second, to call attention to the importance of evaluations and the need to design them well.

*This paper is adapted from a much fuller report by the same authors entitled "Assessing social innovations: an empirical base for policy" appearing as Chapter 2 in Carl A. Bennett and Arthur A. Lumsdaine (Eds.) *Evaluation and Experiment: Some Critical Issues in Assessing Social Programs*, Academic Press, New York, 1975, pp. 39–193 with the permission of the Academic Press.

How do we choose an innovation to include in this review, when there exist currently hundreds of social and socio-medical programs? The answer is that we have restricted our review to include only those innovations that have been well evaluated. By "well evaluated" we mean that a particular sort of field study was part of the innovation—a randomized, controlled field study. Only a small fraction of evaluations fall into this category. Yet we will find later on that evaluations based on less stringent design criteria lead to less assured conclusions.

The studies we review came to us from several sources: a list compiled by Jack Elinson and Cyrille Gell, a list compiled by Robert Boruch, our own list which we have been collecting for years, and finally Bucknam McPeek using the MEDLARS computer-based reference retrieval system provided us with some surgical studies.

If all innovations worked well, the need for evaluations would be less pressing. And if we forecast nearly perfectly, the suggestion might even be made that we were not trying enough new things. Our findings show that this happy state of affairs does not hold; they show, rather, that only a modest fraction of innovations work well. This finding makes clear that innovations need to have their performance assessed. And if society decides to sponsor such assessments, and acts upon their outcomes, designing evaluations that are clearly reliable becomes crucially important.

MEDICAL AND SOCIAL INNOVATIONS

As we studied many of the evaluations that examine social programs, we were struck by how many of the research designs had been taken directly from the methods of agronomy or the natural sciences. But the idea that the exact techniques that have worked so well in agriculture or physics can be directly applied to the evaluation of social programs is naive. Perhaps a much closer parallel to social research comes from medical research, a field that suffers many of the same difficulties that beset the evaluation of social programs. Physicians, in general, and surgeons, in particular, have been diligent in their attempts to evaluate the effects of their therapies on their patients. Indeed, some techniques for implementing and analyzing randomized controlled field trials have been developed in this context. Some examples of problems faced by medical programs that parallel those often faced by social programs are:

- Multiple outcomes and often negative side effects.
- In multi-institutional trials the actual treatments delivered may differ from place to place, although the original intention was to deliver identical treatments in several places.
- Patients often differ in their general condition, in the state of their disease, and in their response to treatment.

- Ethical tensions may exist between study design and the perceived best interests of the patients.
- Patients may adapt their lives so as to minimize their symptoms and thus prevent their disease from being diagnosed.
- Patients may receive additional treatments, unprescribed and un-controlled, that are unknown to the physician and perhaps never discovered.

We feel that the social evaluator will find a closer parallel to his own work in medical and health investigations than in those of the laboratory scientist.

OUR RATINGS OF INNOVATIONS

In our full study from which this essay is adapted, we studied in detail 28 well-evaluated innovations. We present here a sample of these well-evaluated innovations to illustrate the thrust of our findings. An overall summary of all 28 follows.

We rate each innovation according to a five-point scale, from double plus (++), meaning a very successful innovation—it does well some of the major things it was supposed to do; to double minus (--), meaning a definitely harmful innovation. A single minus (-) indicates a slightly harmful or nega-tive innovation. A zero (0) means that the innovation does not seem to have much if any effect in either the positive or negative direction. It could mean also that the innovation has both small positive and small negative effects, neither overwhelming the other. A plus (+) means that the innovation seems to have a somewhat positive effect, but that one would have to weigh parti-cularly carefully whether it was worth its price. We have not carried out detailed cost-benefit analyses here.

The reader might disagree with our ratings, but this worry is not as sub-stantial as one might at first suppose. The reader who wants more information about the individual studies will find it in the full paper [Gilbert et al., 1975] as well as references to the original research reports.

We wish to stress again that *we are not rating the methodology* of the field trial. All of the field trials we discuss were in our judgment of sufficient size and quality to give strong evidence of the efficacy of the innovation. Thus the rating applies to the *innovation* as measured by the field trial.

FIVE EXAMPLES TO ILLUSTRATE THE STUDIES AND THE RATINGS

1. The Salk Vaccine Trials (Francis et al., 1955; Meier, 1972)

The 1954 trial to test a new preventive medication for paralytic polio, the Salk vaccine, is most instructive. First, it exposed children to a new vaccine, and thereby showed that we as a nation have been willing to experiment on people, even our dearest ones, our children. Secondly, the preliminary arguments over the plan instructed us, as did the way it was actually carried out — in two parallel studies.

In the initial design — the *observed control method* — the plan was to give the vaccine to those second graders whose parents volunteered them for the study, to give nothing to the first and third graders, and then to compare the average result for the untreated first and third grade with the treated group in the second grade.

There are troubles here. In the more sanitary neighborhoods, polio occurs more frequently than in unsanitary neighborhoods, and the more sanitary regions are associated with higher income and better education. It is also a social fact that better educated people tend to volunteer more than less well educated ones. Consequently we could expect that the volunteers in the second grade would be more prone to have the diseases in the first place than the average second grader, and than the average of the first and third graders. The comparison might well not be valid because of this bias.

Some state public health officials noticed these difficulties and recommended instead a second design, the *placebo control method*, which randomizes the vaccine among volunteers from all grade groups; that is, these officials recommended a randomized controlled field trial. Half the volunteers got the vaccine and half a salt water injection (placebo), so that the "blindness" of the diagnoses could be protected. Thus the physician could be protected from his expectations for the outcome in making a diagnosis. This meant that the self-selection effects and their associated bias would be balanced between the vaccinated and unvaccinated groups of volunteers, and that the hazards to validity from an epidemic in a grade would be insured against.

In actuality, both methods were used: one in some states and the other in others. The result has been carefully analyzed, and the randomized trial (placebo control) shows conclusively a reduction in paralytic polio rate from about 57 per hundred thousand among the controls to about 16 per hundred thousand in the vaccinated group. (See Table 1.)

In the states where only the second-grade volunteers were vaccinated, the vaccinated volunteers had about the same rate (17 per hundred thousand) as those vaccinated (16 per hundred thousand) in the placebo control areas. The expected bias of an increased rate for volunteers as compared to non-volunteers appeared among the whole group. Among the placebo controls, the volunteers who were not vaccinated had the highest rate (57 per hundred thousand) and those who declined to volunteer had 35 or 36 per hundred thousand. In the states using the observed control method, the first and third graders, who were not asked to volunteer and were not vaccinated, had a rate between the two extremes, 46 per hundred thousand.

Rating: ++

TABLE 1. Summary of Study Cases by Vaccination Status for Salk Vaccine Experiment.

Study group	Study population (thousands)	Paralytic poliomyelitis cases: rate per hundred thousand
Placebo control areas: Total	749	36
Vaccinated	201	16
Placebo	201	57
Not inoculated*	339	36
Incomplete vaccinations	8	12
Observed control areas: Total	1,081	38
Vaccinated	222	17
Controls**	725	46
Grade 2 not inoculated	124	35
Incomplete vaccinations	10	40

*Includes 8,577 children who received one or two injections of placebo.
**First- and third-grade total population.
Source: Paul Meier, 1972; from Table 1, p. 11.

2. The Gamma Globulin Study (U.S. Public Health Service, 1954)

The general success of the Salk vaccine randomized study can be contrasted with the results of a corresponding earlier study of gamma globulin which was carried out in a nonrandomized trial. In 1953, during the summer, 235,000 children were inoculated in the hope of preventing or modifying the severity of poliomyelitis. "The committee recognized that it would be very difficult to conduct rigidly controlled studies in the United States during 1953" (p. 3). They hoped to use mass inoculation in various places and compare differential attack rates at different sites, as well as to analyze other epidemiological data. In the end this approach turned out to be inconclusive, and the authors of that study describe the need for a more carefully controlled experiment.

No Rating: not a randomized study

Why do we introduce this brief reference to a nonrandomized evaluation amidst all the others that we consider well done? Because we consider the contrast between the Salk and the gamma globulin studies particularly striking, and therefore informative. Both studies had, by most standards, very large sample sizes. Yet putting these studies side by side we see that simply having a large number of participants in an evaluation does not imply the results are capable of reliable interpretation. The Salk vaccine study had two investigations in parallel and they support each other. But our confidence in the findings is based primarily on the randomized component of the overall study. This does not help us in a situation where an observed control study is performed alone.

Uncontrolled biases can make interpretation difficult because it becomes necessary for the interpreter to guess the size of the bias, and, when its size may be comparable to that of the treatment effect, the interpreter is guessing the final result.

This is what happend in the gamma globulin study. We must recognize that whether or not gamma globulin was good for the purpose, the lack of randomization undermined the expert investigators' ability to draw firm conclusions, in spite of the large size of the study. The children were put at risk. Although it must be acknowledged that conducting randomized studies would have been difficult in 1953, those who argue today that randomized trials have ethical problems may wish to think about the problems of studies that put the same or greater numbers of people at risk without being able to generate data that can answer the questions being asked.

We now return to several further examples of *well-done* evaluations.

3. Delinquent Girls (Meyer, Borgatta, & Jones, 1965)

The investigators tried to reduce juvenile delinquency among teen-age girls in two ways: first, by predicting which girls were likely to become delinquent; and secondly, by applying a combination of individual and group treatment to girls who exhibited potential problem behaviors. The population was four cohorts of girls entering a vocational high school; of these, approximately one quarter were screened into this study as indicating potential problems. These girls were randomly assigned to a treatment group which was given treatment at Youth Consultation Services (YCS), a social agency; and to a nontreatment (control) group given no special services. The assignments were 189 to YCS, 192 to the nontreatment group.

The result was that in spite of the group and the individual counseling, delinquency was not reduced. The investigators were successful in identifying girls who were likely to become delinquent, but that was not the primary purpose of the study. They report that, "on all the measures . . . grouped together as school-related behavior . . . none of them supplies conclusive evidence of an effect by the therapeutic program" (p. 176). Similar findings were reported for out-of-school behavior.

We view this innovation as rating a zero, though the detection ability might be of value on another occasion.

Rating: 0

4. Probation for Drunk Arrests (Ditman et al., 1967)

Encouraged by preliminary work on the use of probation with suspended sentence as a way of getting chronic drunk offenders into treatment, Ditman et al. developed with the cooperation of the San Diego Municipal Court a randomized controlled field study. Offenders who had had either two drunk arrests in the previous three months or three in the previous year were fined $25, given a 30-day suspended sentence, and then assigned by judges to one of three groups: 1) no treatment, 2) alcoholic clinic, and 3) Alcoholics Anonymous. The primary payoff variables were number of rearrests and time before first rearrest. The total study included 301 individuals, divided randomly into the three groups. The results, based on the 80% of the subjects for whom good records are available, were that the "no treatment" group did as well as or better than the other two groups, which performed practically identically. Table 2 shows the detailed results. Ditman et al. conclude that the study gives no support to a general policy of forced short term referrals, on the basis of the suggestive evidence contained in the paper.

Table 2 shows that 44% of the "no treatment" group had no rearrests (in the first year) as opposed to about 32% in the other groups. Although the missing 20% of the data might change this picture somewhat, the overall result is compelling. (The missing data arise because of difficulty in getting complete data from two distinct sources of records.) Since the difference, though favoring the control, is well within the range of chance effects, we rate this innovation as zero rather than minus.

Rating: 0

TABLE 2.   Number of Drunk Rearrests Among 241 Offenders in Three Treatment Groups.

Treatment Group	Rearrests			
	None	One	Two or More	Total
No treatment	32 (44%)	14 (19%)	27 (37%)	73
Alcoholism clinic	26 (32%)	23 (28%)	33 (40%)	82
Alcoholics Anonymous	27 (31%)	19 (22%)	40 (47%)	86
Total	85	56	100	241

Source: Ditman et al., *American Journal of Psychiatry*, 1967, *124*, 160–63. Copyright © the American Psychiatric Association.

5. Psychiatric After-Care (Sheldon, 1964)

Mental hospitals in England had high readmission rates, so a field study was undertaken to see if "after-care" of discharged patients could reduce readmission significantly. Women between the ages of 20 and 59 were randomly assigned to psychiatric after-care treatment or to their general practitioner, the latter being viewed as the standard treatment. The after-care involved 45

women; the standard involved 44. The psychiatric after-care group was further divided into a day center nurse treatment mode and an outpatient clinic
with a doctor; this assignment was also random.

After six months, the general practioners returned their patients to the
hospital in about 47% of the cases, while the nurse and the MD (the psychiatric team) sent back about 18% of theirs. The psychiatric team kept their
group under care for a longer period than the general practitioners, but had
less rehospitalization. The investigation found that the better the attendance,
the less the readmission in all three groups. But the psychiatric team was
more frequently associated with good attendance by the patient than was
the general practitioner.

We rate this innovation plus. The lower return-to-hospital data make it
seem like a double plus, but since the innovators may be biased in keeping
patients out, we think caution is in order. Were the decision for rehospitalization being made by a separate decision group, the research would be tighter.

Rating: +

SUMMARY OF RATINGS

We hope these several examples illustrate our general procedure.

Table 3 summarizes the ratings of the 28 studies we analyzed in our
original paper. Since the gamma globulin study was not a randomized trial,
we do not include it in the ratings.

Overall, six innovations, or about 21% of the total, were scored double
plus. The rate of double pluses does not differ sharply among the three
groups. The pile-up at zero, 13 out of 28, or 46%, suggests that innovations
that are carefully evaluated yield disappointing results a fair proportion of
the time.

We warn that there may be some upward bias owing to selective reporting and selective finding by our searches. Even so, when we consider the high
rate of failure of laboratory innovations, we can take pleasure in a success
rate as high as the one seen here.

Except for the surgical innovations where we have a rather solid description of our population, the skeptical reader may feel we have no grounds for
discussing rates of successful innovations in the absence of a population and
in the presence of several possible selection effects. The difficulty is not
unique—if one wants to know the percentage of new products that succeed
or the percentage of new businesses that succeed, the same problems of
definition of population and success arise.

Yet we can make some reasonable guesses about direction of bias. First,
evaluations that find a successful innovation are probably more likely to be
written up and published than those which find an innovation to be a failure.
Further, more successful programs are more likely to have come to our
attention in our original review of studies. Consequently, we believe that the

TABLE 3. Summary of Ratings.

Rating	--	-	0	+	++
			3	2	3
Total Social Innovations 8	0	0	D2. Welfare Workers D3. Girls at Voc. High D7. Pretrial Conf.	D4. Cottage Life D6. L.A. Police (or ++)	D1. Neg. Income Tax D5. Manhattan Bail D8. ESAP
		1	4	2	1
Total Socio-medical Innovations 8	0	F1. Kansas Blue-Cross	F3. Comp. Med. Care F4. Drunk Probation F7. Nursing Home F8. Family Medical Care	F5. Psychiatric After-care F6. Mental Illness	F2. Tonsillectomy
	1	1	6	2	2
Total Medical 12	H8. Everting	H10. Yttrium-90	H2. Vagotomy (Cox) H3. Vagotomy (Kennedy) H5. Cancer H6. Portacaval Shunt H9. Chlorhexidine H11. *Gastric Freezing	H4. Bronchus (possibly ++) H7. Ampicillin	H1. Vagotomy (Johnson) H12. *Salk Vaccine
Grand Total 28	1	2	13	6	6

*These two studies did not emerge from the MEDLARS search. All the other medical innovations did.

estimate of about 21% successful innovations is high compared to what a census would yield.

To sum up, the major findings of this table are that 1) among societal innovations studied here, about one in five succeeded; and 2) among those that succeeded, the gain was often small in size, though not in importance.

Both findings have important consequences for the policy maker considering methods of evaluation and for the attitudes toward programs that society needs to develop.

NONRANDOMIZED STUDIES

Now that we have looked at randomized controlled field trials, we explore the results of investigations that for the most part did not use randomization. We will see the consequences of this approach for both weakness of the findings and the ultimate time taken to gather firm information.

We have mentioned earlier the value for social investigators of learning from the medical experience. What we have been observing recently in medicine are systematic attempts to appreciate the interpretative difficulties in ordinary nonrandomized investigations as compared with randomized controlled clinical trials. Much experience is building up, and we can profit from a short review of very extensive work in a few medical areas.

About 1945 an operation called portcaval shunt was introduced to treat bleeding in the esophagus for certain patients, and this operation has been extended for other purposes. After 20 years of experience with this operation and 154 papers on the subject, it still was not clear (Grace, Muench, & Chalmers, 1966) what advice a physician should give to a patient with esophageal varices. Grace, Muench, and Chalmers reviewed the literature to see whether they could resolve such questions as whether the operation would prevent further hemorrhage, what disabling side effects there might be, or what expectation of life went with the operation as compared with not having it.

They rated the investigations on two variables: degree of control in the investigation and degree of enthusiasm for the operation as expressed in the article reporting the trial. The degrees of enthusiasm after the study are: marked, moderate (with some reservations), and no conclusions or enthusiasm. The degrees of control are: 1) well-controlled — random assignment to treatment groups; 2) poorly controlled — selection of patients for treatment (compared with an unselected group or some other experience; and 3) uncontrolled — no comparison with another group of untreated patients.

Table 4 shows clearly that following their uncontrolled studies, investigators almost invariably express some enthusiasm for the shunt, and more than two thirds of the time express marked enthusiasm. Poorly controlled investigations have much the same outcome. On the other hand, in the six instances where the study was well-controlled, three investigators expressed moderate enthusiasm; the rest none. We assume that the investigators using the well-controlled field trials had better grounds for their degree of enthusiasm than did those with no controls or poor controls. (See footnote on Table 4 for more detail on the operations.)

This investigation is informative because we can put the results of uncontrolled, poorly controlled, and well-controlled studies side by side. In all, the results of the investigation show that uncontrolled and poorly controlled studies led to greater enthusiasm than was warranted on the basis of the well-controlled studies. If the poorly controlled studies had suggested conclusions similar to those of the well-controlled trials, we, the surgeons, and policy makers, could be more comfortable with the results of related studies in similar contexts. But we see instead that the results are far from the same. By performing many poorly controlled trials we waste time and human experience and mislead ourselves as well. The argument that sometimes has been advanced that we do not have time to wait for well-controlled trials, because decisions need to be made immediately, does not seem to have been applicable here.

TABLE 4.   Degree of Control Versus Degree of Investigator Enthusiasm for Shunt Operation in 53 Studies Having at Least 10 Patients in the Series.

Degree of control	Degree of enthusiasm			Totals
	Marked	Moderate	None	
Well-controlled	0	3*	3*	6
Poorly controlled	10	3	2	15
Uncontrolled	24	7	1	32
Totals	34	13	6	53

Source: Revised from Grace, Muench, & Chalmers (1966), Table 2, p. 685. Copyright © 1966 The Williams and Wilkins Co., Baltimore.

*In the original source, the cell "well-controlled—moderate enthusiasm" had one entry, but Dr. Chalmers informed us by personal communication that two studies can now be added to that cell. Furthermore, he told us that the "well-controlled—moderate enthusiasm" group is associated with therapeutic shunts, and the "well-controlled—none" with prophylactic shunts.

FINDINGS, INTERPRETATIONS, AND RECOMMENDATIONS

THE RESULTS OF INNOVATIONS. To see how effectively new ideas for helping people worked out in practice, we have collected a series of innovations from social programs and medicine that have been well evaluated. The overall findings are that 1) about a fifth of these programs were clear and substantial successes; 2) a similar number had some small to moderate positive effects; and 3) most of the remaining programs either had no discernible effects or were mixed in their effects, while a few were even found to be harmful rather than beneficial. These proportions do not differ sharply among the social, medical, and socio-medical studies.

How should we interpret these findings? If most innovations had worked, one might well feel that we were not being expansive or broad enough in our attempts to ameliorate social problems. If hardly any had worked, one might conclude that not enough thought and planning were being put into these programs and that they were wasting society's resources. Although our results fall between these two extremes, we would have liked to see a higher proportion of successful innovations, particularly since we feel that the selection biases of our observational study are probably causing the data to overestimate the proportion of successful innovations rather than under-estimate them. Thus it seems to us that the more successful innovations would be both more likely to have been well evaluated and more likely to have come to our attention. If it is true that we are less apt to evaluate programs that are feared to have little effect, society should be concerned that so many very large programs have been evaluated with only nonrandom-ized studies, if at all.

FINDINGS FOR NONRANDOMIZED TRIALS. Although we are often pushed to do them for reasons of expediency, uncontrolled trials and obser-vational studies have frequently been misleading in their results. Such misdirection leads to the evaluations' being ineffective and occasionally even harmful in their role as tools for decision makers. This was well illustrated in the medical studies by Grace et al., and we are concerned because similar troublesome features are present in many evaluations of social programs. Nonrandomized studies may or may not lead to a correct inference, but without other data the suspicion will persist that their results reflect selection effects. This suspicion leads to three difficulties for the decision maker. First, his confidence in the evaluation is limited, and even when he does believe in the result, he may be reluctant or unable to act because others are not con-vinced by the data. Second, because of this lingering suspicion, observational studies are rarely successful in resolving a controversy about causality. Though controversy about policy implications may of course persist, few controversies about the effects of new programs survive a series of carefully designed randomized controlled trials. Third, nonrandomized studies are not simply neutral in their effects; they may be *harmful* if they result in the *postponement* of randomized studies.

BENEFICIAL SMALL EFFECTS. The observation that few programs have slam-bang effects stresses the importance of measuring small effects reliably. Once small effects are found and documented, it may be possible to build improvements upon them. The banking and insurance businesses have built their fortunes on small effects — effects the size of interest rates. Ten percent per year doubles the principal in a little over seven years. Similarly, a small effect that can be cumulated over several periods—for example, the school life of a student—has the potential of mounting up into a large gain. Natural-ly, small effects require stronger methods for their accurate detection than do large ones. One must be sure that the observed effects are not due to initial differences between groups, or to other spurious causes. Randomized controlled field trials are virtually essential for controlling these sources of bias, and so are necessary for the accurate measurement of small effects.

CONTROLLED TRIALS VS. FOOLING AROUND. Ethical problems have often been cited as reasons for not carrying out well-controlled studies. This is frequently a false issue. The basic question involves comparing the ethics of gathering information systematically about our large scale programs with the ethics of haphazardly implementing and changing treatments as so routinely happens in education, welfare, and other areas. Since the latter approach generates little reliable information, it is unlikely to provide lasting benefits. Although they must be closely monitored, like all investigations involving human subjects, we believe randomized controlled field trials can give society valuable information about how to improve its programs. Conducting such investigations is far preferable to the current practice of "fooling around with people," without their informed consent.

PROBLEMS

1. Why is it true that forecasting the success of social innovations very well could lead to a reluctance to try new things?

2. The authors point out that their technique for selecting studies to study probably leads, if anything, to an *overestimation* of the success of social innovations. Explain why this is so.

3. (a) Explain the rating system the authors use for social innovations.
   (b) Does the methodology of an experiment affect its rating? Explain.

4. If your class were asked for volunteers to participate in a study of grade averages, how would you expect the grade averages of the volunteer group to compare with those of the class as a whole? Explain.

5. Explain the difference between the *observed control method* and the placebo control method in the Salk vaccine trials. Which method is superior and why?

6. What do the authors mean by "blindness" in their discussion of the Salk vaccine trials?

7. Consider Table 1. In the placebo control areas, approximately how many cases of poliomyelitis were there among those fully vaccinated?

8. Explain in some detail, and in contrast to the Salk vaccine trials, the methodological weaknesses of the gamma globulin study.

9. Consider Table 2.

(a) What percentage of the 241 people in the study had no rearrests?

(b) What percentage of those with 2 or more rearrests had received no treatment?

10. In the psychiatric after-care experiment, the innovators (psychiatric team) also made the decision to return patients to the hospital.

(a) Why does this affect the rating of this experiment?

(b) How does this situation differ from the delinquent girls experiment? (Hint: Who decides whether the girls become delinquent?)

11. Consider Table 3. What percentage of the overall number of studies looked at showed that the innovation had at least a somewhat positive effect? What percentage, of the social innovations only, had a negative effect?

12. How did the outcomes of the controlled and uncontrolled investigations of the portacaval shunt operation differ? What are the implications of this difference for social policy makers?

REFERENCES

K. S. Ditman, G. G. Crawford, E. W. Forgy, H. Moskowitz, and C. MacAndrew. 1967. "A Controlled Experiment on the Use of Court Probation for Drunk Arrests." *American Journal of Psychiatry*. 124, pp. 160–163.

Thomas Francis, Jr., et al. 1955. "An Evaluation of the 1954 Poliomyelitis Vaccine Trials—Summary Report." *American Journal of Public Health*. 45:5, pp. 1–63.

J. P. Gilbert, R. J. Light, and F. Mosteller. 1975. "Assessing Social Innovations: An Empirical Basis for Policy." C. A. Bennett and A. A. Lumsdaine, eds., *Evaluation and Experiment: Some Critical Issues in Assessing Social Programs*. New York: Academic Press.

N. D. Grace, H. Muench, and T. C. Chalmers. 1966. "The Present Status of Shunts for Portal Hypertension in Cirrhosis." *Gastroenterology* 50, pp. 684–691.

Paul Meier. 1972. "The Biggest Health Experiment Ever: The 1954 Field Trial of the Salk Poliomyelitis Vaccine." J. M. Tanur et al., eds., *Statistics: A Guide to the Unknown*. San Francisco: Holden-Day.

Meyer, H. J., Borgatta, E. F., and Jones, W. C. *Girls at vocational high: An experiment in social work intervention*. New York: Russell Sage Foundation, 1965.

Sheldon, A. An evaluation of psychiatric after-care. *British Journal of Psychiatry*, 1964, *110*, 662–667.

DO SPEED LIMITS REDUCE TRAFFIC ACCIDENTS?

Frank A. Haight   *Pennsylvania Transportation and Traffic Safety Center*

IT IS surprisingly difficult to discover what factors cause increases or decreases in traffic accidents. Sometimes changes are made in speed limits, in highway design, in driver-licensing standards, or in vehicle specifications in an attempt to decrease accidents. Yet, it can sometimes happen that the number of accidents will actually increase. These surprising increases may come merely from increases in population, or from increases in number of vehicles on the road, or perhaps from greater distances traveled.

MEASURING ACCIDENT RATES

So it is sensible to measure accident *rates* rather than the raw number of accidents. Of course, there is a variety of such rates; among the most common are *accidents per person in the population, accidents per registered vehicle,* and *accidents per vehicle mile traveled.* For example, if along a certain highway there were 500 accidents in 1970 and 10 million vehicle miles, then the last rate would be 50 accidents per million vehicle miles. Often these rates are measured in terms of fatalities rather than in terms of all accidents.

The behavior of these rates in the U.S. since the late thirties has been approximately as follows: (1) the fatality rate per person is increasing slightly; (2) the fatality rate per registered vehicle is decreasing; and (3) the fatality rate per vehicle mile is decreasing, rather quickly during the forties and fifties and less quickly later. From 1963 to 1970 it may even have been stationary. This combination of rates would be consistent with a trend of proportionately more cars but relatively safer ones. This is roughly true also for other places in the world where road traffic plays an important part in the society: Western Europe, Australia, and New Zealand.

The total size of the population considered affects the stability of all such accident rates. For a large country like the United States there is very little fluctuation from year to year or even from month to month because we are dealing with averages based upon large numbers of cars and large numbers of accidents. In a small town, to take the other extreme, it may be nearly impossible to "see the forest for the trees" since a very few accidents may have the effect of changing the average greatly.

This tendency is shown clearly by the data of Figure 1 from the National

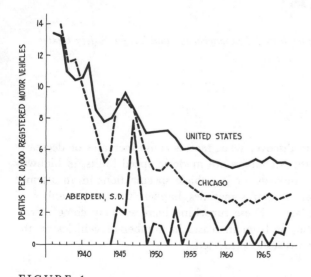

FIGURE 1

Deaths per 10,000 registered motor vehicles, 1936–69, U.S. and selected localities. Source: Data from National Safety Council

Safety Council.   It should be noted that the rate given in Figure 1 is *fatalities per ten thousand registered vehicles*.   A similar graph based on the rate of *fatalities per hundred million vehicle miles driven* would be even more informative, but this rate is not known for subdivisions smaller than whole states. The reason is that the estimate of vehicle miles traveled is based on gasoline consumption and records of this type are not usually kept by municipalities. (Thus, if you buy a gallon of gasoline and throw it away without using it in your car, you will actually lower the fatality rate per vehicle mile for that year as much as if you had used the gas safely in your car!)   Because the averages for the country are so stable but those of small towns so unstable, predictions of the number of fatalities expected over holiday weekends are usually given for the country as a whole rather than for smaller geographical divisions.

EVALUATING CHANGES IN ACCIDENT RATES

From the point of view of accident prevention there are two important consequences of this variability.   The first is that since the most commonly used rate is generally going down, its decrease after some specific change is made does not by itself prove that the change was beneficial.   Second, if the change takes place over a small population—even as small as several million—it may be well nigh impossible to separate the effect of this change from the general chance fluctuation.   The statistical point is not really the population size, but the general level of the numbers of accidents.   The numbers of accidents do not vary much percentagewise when the general level is large, but they do when it is small (see the essay by Campbell).

An added difficulty is that most changes in traffic patterns, laws, or law enforcement are expensive: rebuilding highways, eliminating grade crossings, building safer cars, and enforcing safety rules are typically costly items.   Some of these factors are, in addition, nearly permanent; once done it is not easy to undo them.   For example, if an expensive bridge is built, it cannot readily be relocated.   Hence, there is a tendency to introduce improvements in the road system on the basis of good sense and experience rather than on empirically demonstrated improvements in highway safety; many claims of benefit are to be taken in a general rather than specific sense—the accident rate *is* decreasing although it is hard to pinpoint the exact causes.

This may in some ways be a gratifying situation, but it is not helpful in planning new measures.   Given a fixed budget, should investment be made in driver training, in better enforcement of traffic regulations, in alcohol testing, in road reconstruction, in speed limit changes, or in some completely different approach such as subsidizing public transit?   Furthermore, safety and budget are not the only considerations; convenience counts too.   How can we find out if each of these proposed measures is effective?

EXPERIMENTS TO EVALUATE PROPOSED CHANGES

It would seem that a logical method would be to set up an experiment. But, in field after field of public policy, responsible authorities object to carefully controlled experimentation because they feel they cannot tamper with such important and expensive arrangements. Although there is much to discuss on this point, we shall not debate the rights and wrongs of it here, but report only that road authorities are usually unwilling to have the road transport system play the role of a guinea pig. They regard it as expensive and confusing to the traveling public and likely to be inconclusive.

Nevertheless, let us think about how such an experiment to test the effect of an improvement in traffic control on accident fatalities should be designed. Because fatal accidents are rare (less than six fatalities per 100 million vehicle miles in the U.S., for example), a large sample of driving is needed for such an experiment to give a clear answer through the mist of chance fluctuation. Furthermore, to allow for a general decreasing trend in rates the statistician would like to have the proposed improvement operate only on alternate days of the week or be "turned on and off" according to some reliable, recognizable program. The policeman will usually not agree to have traffic regulations change so often, although he may be willing to experiment for a week or two along a few miles of highway.

THE SCANDINAVIAN EXPERIMENT

An exception to this usual official reluctance to experiment has been in progress in Denmark and Sweden for nearly ten years. The governments of these countries have introduced *periodic speed limits* (speed limits that stay the same for long periods of time over long stretches of road, and then are changed for other long periods).

We must realize that speed limits of any sort are bitterly opposed in many European countries and are considered to be justified only if their reduction of accident rates can be strictly demonstrated. The American idea that speed limits are favorable for all aspects of road usage (for example, maximum flow), not merely safety, is in general not accepted.

In Sweden, a royal commission was established in 1961 to investigate various aspects of speed control; the commission members were statisticians and other scientists from the country's foremost technical university. The experiment for the first year involved the comparison of a 90-kilometer-per-hour limit (about 56.7 miles per hour) against no speed limit over 71 different road sections, chosen to represent a variety of road conditions. In that first year the speed limitation was in force from Friday, May 19, through Wednesday, May 24, from Thursday, June 22, through Wednesday, July 12, and from Friday, September 1, through Monday, September 11.

In subsequent years, the experimental program has been more ambitious and more complicated, involving speed limits of 90 kph, 110 kph, and 130 kph, as well as larger road networks; in 1968, all the roads of the European highway system in Sweden were included, together with some of the principal national main roads. Also the speed limits (or lack of limits) were maintained for longer periods of time, sometimes several months or a year, in order to obtain larger samples of accidents.

ACCIDENT RATES AND THE POISSON PROCESS

With the immense quantity of data obtained (7000 accidents during the 1968 experiment, for example) many different types of statistical analysis were performed. This article deals with one analysis which evoked some theoretical problems: before-and-after comparisons of accident rates.

Long study of the traffic accident phenomenon shows that a simple random process which well describes the instant at which accidents occur is the so-called *Poisson process*. A Poisson process is a quantitative way of expressing the fact that the accidents are indeed *accidental,* that is, that each accident occurs at a moment in time which is completely independent of the moments when other accidents occur—the times of the accidents are perfectly scrambled. This specification is incomplete, however, unless it also includes a so-called mean value that expresses how often accidents occur *on the average.* There can be a Poisson accident process on a main highway with, for example, 100 accidents per year on the average, or on a small rural road with only one accident per year on the average. In such a case the accident record for the rural road for 100 years would, if compressed into a year, duplicate the statistical properties of the single year on the main road. Thus, if we let the letter m denote the mean number of accidents observed for a section of road, we find that m will depend (among other things) on the traffic volume characteristic of the road sections. In the Swedish experiments, the volumes ranged from less than 150 vehicles per day up to values in excess of 5000 per day.

This variability in the traffic volume typical of a road section was complicated further by variability in volume over the days of the year. Some roads have heavy traffic during the summer, others in the winter. On certain days there are special events such as football games or national holidays to increase traffic flow. The weather influences both the volume of traffic and the risk of an accident, and even if the record is limited to the same day in consecutive years, there may have been a blizzard on one of these days and not on the other.

Therefore, the problem of comparing values of m without the speed limit to values of m with a speed limit seems to break down into thousands of special tests, one for each bit of road and bit of time. Fragmentation of the problem in this way reduces the sample sizes and seems to nullify the whole purpose of the experiment. Also, the conclusions would be far less reliable because of the small samples, and in the majority of cases, it might be impossible to come to any conclusion whatsoever.

It is clearly desirable to group the road segments and days into larger groups that will be homogeneous, but the factors involved are so varied as to make this nearly impossible. How can we compare the effect of a rain-shower with that of a construction project, or of a national holiday with an extra-wide shoulder? Is there any quantitative equivalence between a road in the far north experiencing wintry conditions for long periods and one near a ferry terminal serving many foreign tourists?

The solution to this problem was found to lie in grouping together road segments having the same number of accidents during the total period of the study, and for each group examining the proportion of accidents that occurred in the "before" period, and the complementary proportion that occurred during the "after" period; these time periods are of equal length. Thus, for example, we group together all road segments having ten accidents over the total experimental period; these road segments might be very different, yet their qualitative differences balance out to the extent that they experienced the same overall number of accidents.

To get an intuitive idea about the reasoning, let us suppose that there are but two conditions: having a speed limit and not having one. If we suppose that having a speed limit is effective in improving safety, then when we collect all the road segments we should find that more accidents occur under the "no limit" condition than under the "speed limit" condition. We have many segments, so we can look at the results for many similar segments, and thus pile up a considerable record. Furthermore, in some segments, the "speed limit" condition would have come first, and in others second, and we can check whether the order mattered. We can also see whether "speed limits" matter more to safety in segments with high accident rates or with low, and so on.

In any case, the key statistical technique was to put together those road segments having the same total number of accidents in the "before" and "after" periods, even though the segments grouped together might have nothing in common beyond their accident experience. With this approach, it was found that deciding whether the Poisson mean value m had changed as a result of the speed limit could be reduced to a simpler statistical problem involving the ratio of the m value "before" to the m value "after," given that the total accidents "before-and-after" was the same.

SOME RESULTS

One general result of the Swedish and Danish analyses is especially interesting. It appears that speed limits were more effective in Sweden than in Denmark! The reason behind this is not at all clear.

We can only speculate on the value of a similar experiment in the U.S. Probably it would not be useful to choose "speed limit" as the experimental variable because most of our communities have roughly similar attitudes towards speed restriction, with relatively small local variations.   A more interesting variable might be vehicle inspection systems, which vary greatly from no compulsory inspection at all in California to very rigorous periodic checks in Pennsylvania.   There has been recent discussion in technical journals about the effect of inspection laws on accident experience.   How could we design an experiment that would test this factor in isolation from others?   We could, perhaps, trace the accidents which Pennsylvania vehicles have on California roads and vice versa.   Or we might begin an inspection system which applies only to blue cars and trace the proportion of blue cars in accidents.   Either of these, or some other design, would give some clear indication of the usefulness of various inspection systems.

PROBLEMS

1. Why is it more reasonable to consider accident rates, rather than the actual number of accidents?

2. How has the fatality rate per vehicle mile changed between the 1930's and 1970? Can you speculate on some explanations? (Hint: How large were the road systems and the number of automobiles in the 1930's?)

3. In Figure 1, why does Aberdeen, S.D., show the sharpest increases and decreases in deaths?

4. Considering Figure 1, was the death rate per 10,000 registered vehicles larger for Chicago or the United States as a whole in 1949? In 1945?

5. Why does the author say when commenting on the rate given in Figure 1: "A similar graph based on the rate of *fatalities per hundred million vehicle miles driven* would be even more informative"?

6. Explain how you think number of vehicle miles travelled is estimated from gasoline consumption.

7. If, after a specific safety measure is instituted, the accident rate continues to decline, can this decline be attributed to the safety measure? Explain.

8. The advantages of experimenting to identify measures which reliably reduce the fatality rates are clear. Why haven't more such experiments been done?

9. Why is the Poisson process important for the study of accident rates?

10. In the Scandinavian experiment, what was m? On what did it depend?

11. (a) In the Scandinavian experiment, why couldn't the road segments be grouped by traffic volume?

(b) How were the road segments finally grouped? How did this treat their differences?

12. Can you think of any explanations of why speed limits in Sweden might be more effective than in Denmark?

ELECTION NIGHT ON TELEVISION

Richard F. Link   *Artronic Information Systems, Inc., and Princeton University*

DURING THE evening of the first Tuesday in November in even-numbered years, millions of people all over the U.S. watch the election shows provided by the three major networks. The viewers see a rapid tabulation of the votes cast for the major state offices of senator and governor, and in years when a president is elected, a rapid tabulation of the presidential vote by state and for the nation. They also see a tabulation of the vote for the members of the House of Representatives. They usually hear an announcement of the winner after only a few percent of the vote has been reported, often within minutes of the closing of the polls. As the evening progresses they are treated to analyses that explain how a given candidate won, that is, where his strength and weakness lay, and why it appeared that he won.

Massive machinery operates behind this effort. This machinery is physical in the sense that it requires a very elaborate communications network and extensive usage of computers, but it is also statistical and mathematical in the sense that it requires rapid summaries and interpretations so that the findings can quickly be passed to the viewing public.

We shall not attempt to describe the complete organization necessary to produce the election night show, but we shall describe the three parts of the show that lean most heavily upon computer and statistical technology: vote tabulation, projection of winners, and detailed analysis of the vote. The vote tabulation system is basically the same for all networks, but they differ in their methods for projecting winners and in their analysis of the vote. We shall describe in this paper only the method of projection used by one network (NBC), at least until 1970 when this was written.

Before discussing the procedures and methods used today, we shall give a brief history of the reporting of election night results to give a feel for why and how today's shows came about.

A BRIEF HISTORY OF ELECTION REPORTING

Persons living in the United States, as in other free societies that hold elections, have always had an intense interest in the outcome of elections. Most intense for the elections that involve the presidency, it is reasonably high for gubernatorial and senatorial elections, and at least the numbers of Republicans and Democrats composing the House of Representatives are of concern, even though the election of a particular member usually does not have national significance.

Thus election results have always been news of great interest. Until about 1928, this news reached the public via their newspapers. In general the coverage was relatively slow and incomplete. Radio changed this situation, and election reporting was speeded up. For example, radio reported the upset victory of Harry S. Truman in the early hours following election day in November 1948. Television began to report elections on a national scale in 1952 and has increased its scope and coverage and speed of gathering the vote since then. Extensive primary coverage was introduced during the presidential year of 1964 and continues to be a feature of television reporting today even in "off years" such as 1970.

Speed of coverage is influenced by two factors: the speed with which the vote is obtained from its source (basically a precinct), and then the speed with which it is reported. The speed of reporting the vote, once collected, was greatly increased by reporting via radio as opposed to reporting via newspaper. This reporting speed has not been particularly increased by television, since both radio and television are capable of essentially instantaneous reporting. The speed of vote collection, however, has been greatly increased by the television networks. It is worth reviewing the collection procedures utilized in the past and today.

The U.S. has approximately 175,000 precincts. In the official electoral machinery, the precinct vote is usually forwarded to a county collection center, and then to a state center, often to the Secretary of State there, who then certifies the official vote. Final official collection and certification often take several months. The precinct vote, however, is forwarded to the county level fairly rapidly, perhaps by phone or courier, and the vote at the county level is often quickly available on an unofficial basis. The job of collecting the vote at the county level is much less arduous than that of collecting at the precinct level since there are only about 3000 counties in the country. The vote can be collected faster, nonetheless, if it is collected at the precinct level, and this is the basic innovation that television introduced to vote collection. The networks with their large economic resources were instrumental in establishing a mechanism for obtaining the vote at the precinct level, and communicating it by phone to a central location where it could be processed by a computer.

Competition by television networks in the area of extensive vote collection became very intense by the primary elections of 1964. That year, the New Hampshire primary saw all three of the major television networks collecting and reporting the vote at the precinct level. In fact, some wags have said that there were more television workers in New Hampshire during the 1964 primary than voters, or to put it another way, that it would have been cheaper to bring the New Hampshire voters to New York to vote at a central location, than to collect the vote in New Hampshire. Needless to say, these remarks are exaggerated, but they do indicate the magnitude of the expense involved. The competition in collection became more intense that spring, and culminated in the reporting of the California presidential primary where each of the three networks collected the vote in the more than 30,000 precincts in California. This enormous expense brought only a mixed blessing. The newspaper wire services continued to collect and report the vote in the traditional manner, from complete county returns, so that on the day after the election, after the television networks had reported Goldwater the winner, the newspapers all showed Rockefeller with a substantial lead. The reason for this disparity was that Los Angeles county, with approximately a third of the precincts in the state, did not have a complete county report until too late to meet the newspaper deadlines, and Goldwater ran very strongly in Los Angeles.

This confusion was coupled with another, arising from the fact that each network would report its own vote totals at any instant of time, and, since they were being collected independently, at any given moment their totals were all different. All this led to the formation of an organization called the News Election Service (NES) whose sole purpose is to collect the vote and report it to its members. This service was formed by a cooperative effort of the three television networks (ABC, CBS, NBC) and the two wire services (AP, UPI).

We next examine briefly the operation of the News Election Service.

THE NEWS ELECTION SERVICE

The news election service was formed to provide a uniform and consistent report of the vote to the American public. The figures obtained by this organization are released to its members simultaneously, so that at any instant all networks and news services are able to report the same basic data to the public.

The massive operation functions in the following manner. Reporters, called stringers, are on duty at more than 100,000 of the largest of the 175,000 precincts in the country and at each of the 3000 county reporting centers. These reporters collect the vote at the precinct and county levels and then phone this vote to a central location, adding enough information to identify the source of the report. The vote information is then put into a computer, which checks to see that it appears valid; for example, if it is a precinct report, it checks to see that the vote does not exceed registration in that precinct, or if a county report, that the number of precincts in the county has not been exceeded. Because registration figures and data on number of precincts are not exactly accurate at this time the check depends upon a statistical tolerance rather than an absolute cut-off. Once the report has been checked, if it is a precinct report it is added to the precinct results already reported for that county. If it is a county report, it replaces the previous county report (the county reports are made on a cumulative basis). At regular intervals the computer generates a vote report for each election race for each county in the state and also provides a state total for the presidential, senatorial, and gubernatorial races and a national total for the presidential race. The summary report is generated by comparing the county votes from the county reports with the votes in the county calculated from the precinct reports. It uses the larger figure for the county figure, and then sums over the counties in the state to obtain a state figure. In presidential years an additional summation is made over the states to obtain a national vote figure for the presidency. In addition to providing summary vote totals, percentages for each candidate are reported, as is the fraction of precincts reporting. Similar accumulations are made for house races, but they are organized on a congressional district basis.

Once the information has been calculated, the computer releases the information to its clients. It provides this information in printed form both at the computer location and at the television studio, and it also makes the information available via telephone lines that can be used for input into the various network computer systems.

Extensive research must be done before the election not only to train the stringers, but also to gather the registration figures for the precincts, to find the number of precincts in each county, and to collect other basic data.

This information is essential for the checking process, and for accurate reporting of the fraction of the vote that has been counted.

Extensive preparation must also go into the operation that gets the vote into the computer and into the preparation of the computer to accept the vote, add it properly, and report it correctly. The general name of the operation that prepares the computer to work properly is called coding. Its importance cannot be underestimated. In 1968, mistakes made in the instructions for the computer caused the computer to malfunction, and the vast stream of votes from NES dried up to a trickle shortly after midnight (EST) election night. This malfunction was partly responsible for the uncertainty about the winner in the presidential race, which was not reported by the television networks until Wednesday morning.

This brings us to an area which is still the subject of intensive competition among the three networks. Although they are all constrained to report the same vote totals, they are not constrained in the interpretation of these vote totals; for although the vote total at any instant in time may be interesting in itself, the real interest in an election lies in who wins, in how much he wins by, and in why he wins.

PROJECTING ELECTION WINNERS

The rapid collection and reporting of the vote requires a great deal of organization, computer capability, and communication equipment. All that activity, nonetheless, goes simply to adding the vote up. The question for the election forecaster always remains "When can I be reasonably sure I have tabulated enough of the vote to decide who will be the ultimate winner?"

An easy answer to that question is "Wait until all the votes are counted," but this may take days. Statistical theory, however, sometimes allows us to give an answer earlier. Sometimes it allows us to determine the winner of an election when only a fraction of one percent of the vote has been reported to the analyst. It happens frequently that projections can be made on the basis of information collected by the network and available to the analysts in the television studio before a single vote has been posted for the television audience, because NES has not yet produced vote totals (which, by agreement are the only ones that can be released to the public).

The projection of election night winners requires a combination of historical information, statistical theory for the construction of an appropriate mathematical model of the vote and for deciding when one is sure enough to make a projection, and the actual election night vote. The networks have different schemes for projecting winners, but all of these schemes have the basic elements we have described. We next describe the general scheme used by one network, NBC. We first discuss the projection of the winner in a state race, then the projection of a winner in a presidential election, and finally the projection of the composition of the House of Representatives.

STATE RACES

The information for projecting the winner of a state race comes from three separate sources. First, there is an estimate of the percentage each candidate will get, which is available before election day. This information comes from public opinion polls, from newspaper reporters, from politicians in the state, and similar sources. This initial estimate is often quite accurate and may give a definite indication of how the race is likely to turn out. A second source of information comes from the vote of specially selected precincts the network collects in addition to the vote that NES collects. Typically, there will be 50 to 150 such precincts for each state. Thus nationally a network may have a precinct collection system which has reporters in over 5000 precincts and is completely independent of the NES effort. These precincts are carefully investigated and their voting behavior in past elections is carefully analyzed. Finally, the information from NES is available at a county level.

The information from these three sources is ordered in time. The initial estimate is obviously available first, since it is available before election day. The vote of the special precincts, called *key precincts,* which the networks collect themselves is usually the first vote information available to the network. By the agreement forming NES, this information cannot be used to tabulate the vote, that is, to show to the public, but it can be used to project winners. Often if a race is one-sided, the vote in the initial precincts to come in from the network collection system is sufficient to allow the projection of a winner.

If the race is close, however, more of the special precincts are needed before a winner may be projected, and often it is necessary to use the county information available from NES.

To use the information from the counties, it is necessary to develop a mathematical model. The reason is that different counties have different voting behaviors. For example, New York City is always more Democratic in its vote than the rest of the State of New York. The difference in voting behavior in terms of relative Democratic or Republican leanings can be incorporated into a mathematical model.

The statistical model uses the voting patterns from the recent past. For example, the fraction of the New York State vote in New York City is typically 0.4, and the fraction in the rest of the state 0.6. In a typical past election for governor the Democratic candidate got 50% of the vote in New York City and 40% of the vote in the rest of the state. His statewide vote, then, was $0.4\ (50\%) + 0.6\ (40\%) = 44\%$. Thus New York City was 6% more Democratic than the state average, and the rest of the state was 4% less

Democratic than the state average. This fact can be incorporated into a model so that in this simplest instance, if in a new election the early returns from New York City show 54% for the Democratic candidate and the rest of the state shows 48% for the Democratic candidate, the state projection in percent would be $0.4(54\%) + 0.6(48\%) = 50.4\%$. This indicates that the Democratic candidate would win, although if the returns were very early, this projection would not be considered sufficiently accurate to make an announcement of a victory.

Another factor considered in the statistical model is whether the fraction of the vote assigned to the various parts of the state is accurate for this election. If it snowed heavily in upstate New York, but not in New York City, and cut the vote upstate, but not in New York City, the fraction of the vote in the election might be 0.5 for New York City and 0.5 for the rest of the state; that is, the relative voter turnout in New York City would be higher than normal. In this case the projection would be $0.5(54\%) + 0.5(48\%) = 51\%$, indicating a better chance for Democratic victory. Thus the differential turnout must also be considered in the model in order to make vote projections.

The use of computers allows such a model to be constructed using detailed information for all the counties of a state rather than just the two regions in our example, to provide not only a projection, but also an indication of the accuracy of the projection, so that one can decide when a projection may safely be announced.

It is useful for the model to include the prior estimate available to the network, and results for the special key precincts, so that all information available to the network is effectively utilized. Such a model sometimes allows the results of a race to be called with near certainty, even though only a small fraction of the vote is reported, and the race is relatively close.

It is network policy not to predict the winner unless it is almost a certainty that the predicted winner will actually win. The accuracy of the predictions can be gauged by the fact that, during a given evening when over a hundred predictions may be made, there is usually at most one mistake. The use of such models, developed by statistical theory, allows the networks to enforce their policy, and at the same time "call" close races, because the precision of the estimates developed by the models is always known. One of the most important outputs of the statistical model in this decision problem, as in many others, is the estimated precision of the result.

PRESIDENTIAL RACE

Part of the output of the models used in the calling of state races is the percentage of the vote each candidate is likely to get, as well as an indication as to the accuracy of that percentage. This information is also available for all states for presidential races. (Note that for some states early in the evening the only information available is the preelection estimate.) In this case, however, the percentages are not the final output of the model, but only necessary information to feed into another model whose purpose is to project the winner of the presidential race. The outcome for each state must be utilized in an electoral college model to project the winner of the presidency. This model also provides an estimate of precision, so that the accuracy of the estimate can be assessed, and again the correctness of the prediction can be evaluated.

The loss of the NES vote totals in 1968 held up the projection of the presidential winner because the race was very close in several important states, and the prior and precinct information was not sufficient to make an early responsible projection of the winner.

HOUSE RACES

A projection of the composition of the House of Representatives requires a model similar to the one used for projection of presidential races, the main difference being that each house seat counts as 1, the prior estimates are ordinarily less reliable than those for states in presidential elections, and the vote is only reported by house district. In addition to the projection and vote information, the networks also provide an analysis of the vote. This is the next topic that we shall consider.

NEWS ANALYSIS

We have seen that there is a vast reservoir of information available to the network on election night. The networks utilize this information for vote tabulation and to project winners, but they also make more detailed breakdowns of the information to analyze the election results in depth.

The networks often organize the vote by areas in the state; these areas may be geographical or they may be demographic, for example, showing separately the urban, suburban, and rural vote. The percentage for each candidate can be calculated for each of these categories.

In addition to this detailed inspection of the vote, the networks often collect additional precinct information from precincts that they have tagged as having a high concentration of certain types of voters. Tags that have been used are ethnic (such as Italian, Jewish, Catholic), racial (such as Black), economic (such as high, middle, or low socioeconomic status), rural, and so on. These analyses add a great deal of background and some insight to the reporting of the vote.

CONCLUSION

The reporting effort of the television networks represents an area of activity that could not exist without the computer and without modern statistics. It represents a blend of modern technology and the traditional skills of the reporter.

The statistical techniques of vote projection may have other applications. For example, it might be possible by similar methods to establish the pattern of yields of corn county by county in Iowa from historical records, and accurately to estimate the state yield from the yields of only a few early harvesting counties.

PROBLEMS

1. What are the three parts of the election night show which rely most heavily on computer and statistical technology?

2. What are the advantages of precinct level vote collection by the media? The disadvantages?

3. Why was the NES formed? Does this mean that the only data available to the networks is from the NES?

4. Statistical theory enters into winner projection in two ways. Describe them.

5. What is a "key precinct"? Are they the same for all networks?

6. The gubernatorial candidate in New York is assured of 60% of the New York City vote and 50% in the rest of the state. As stated in this article, the New York City vote usually represents 40% of the statewide total. What percentage of the total vote can our candidate expect?

7. Our candidate is dismayed. A sudden blizzard has hit New York City on the first Tuesday in November, cutting the city's voter turnout to 30% of the state total. Can the candidate still win?

8. Why is the precision of an estimate important in winner projection?

9. Besides the estimated voting percentages themselves, what is an equally important output of the projection models discussed in the article?

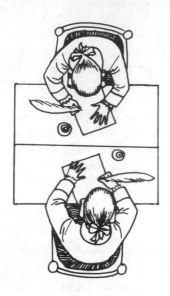

DECIDING AUTHORSHIP

Frederick Mosteller   *Harvard University*

David L. Wallace   *University of Chicago*

ART, MUSIC, literature, the social, biological, and physical sciences share a common need to classify things: What artist painted the picture? Who composed the piece? Who wrote the document? If paroled, will the prisoner repeat his crime? What disease does the patient have? What trace chemical is damaging the process? In the field of statistics, we call these questions classification or discrimination problems.

Questions of authorship are frequent and sometimes important. Most people have heard of the Shakespeare-Bacon-Marlowe controversy over who wrote the great plays usually attributed to Shakespeare. A less well-known but carefully studied question deals with the authorship of a number of Christian religious writings called the Paulines, some being books in the New Testament: Which ones were written by Paul and which by others? In many authorship questions the solution is easy once we set about counting some-

thing systematically.   But we treat here an especially difficult problem from
American history, the controversy over the authorship of the 12 *Federalist*
papers claimed by both Alexander Hamilton and James Madison, and we
show how a statistical analysis can contribute to the resolution of historical
questions.

The Federalist papers were published anonymously in 1787–88 by Alexander Hamilton, John Jay, and James Madison to persuade the citizens of the
State of New York to ratify the Constitution.   Seventy-seven papers appeared
as letters in New York newspapers over the pseudonym "Publius."   Together
with eight more essays, they were published in book form in 1788 and have
been republished repeatedly both in the U.S. and abroad.   *The Federalist*
remains today an important work in political philosophy.   It is also the leading
source of information for studying the intent of the framers of the Constitution, as, for example, in recent decisions on congressional reapportionment,
since Madison had taken copious notes at the Constitutional Convention.

It was generally known who had written *The Federalist*, but no public
assignment of specific papers to authors occurred until 1807, three years after
Hamilton's death as a result of his duel with Aaron Burr.   Madison made
his listing of authors only in 1818 after he had retired from the Presidency.   A
variety of lists with conflicting claims have been disputed for a century and
a half.   There is general agreement on the authorship of 70 papers—5 by
Jay, 14 by Madison, and 51 by Hamilton.   Of the remaining 15, 12 are
in dispute between Hamilton and Madison, and 3 are joint works to a disputed
extent.   No doubt the primary reason the dispute exists is that Madison and
Hamilton did not hurry to enter their claims.   Within a few years after writing
the essays, they had become bitter political enemies and each occasionally
took positions opposing some of his own *Federalist* writings.

The political content of the essays has never provided convincing evidence
for authorship.   Since Hamilton and Madison were writing a brief in favor
of ratification, they were like lawyers working for a client; they did not need
to believe or endorse every argument they put forward favoring the new
Constitution.   While this does not mean that they would go out of their
way to misrepresent their personal positions, it does mean that we cannot
argue "Hamilton wouldn't have said that because he believed otherwise."
And, as we have often seen, personal political positions change.   Thus the
political content of a disputed essay cannot give strong evidence in favor
of Hamilton's or of Madison's having written it.

The acceptance of the various claims by historians has tended to change
with political climate.   Hamilton's claims were favored during the last half
of the 19th century, Madison's since then.   While the thorough historical
studies of the historian Douglass Adair over the past several decades support
the Madison claims, the total historical evidence is today not much different
from that which historians like the elder Henry Cabot Lodge interpreted as

favoring Hamilton. New evidence was needed to obtain definite attributions, and internal statistical stylistic evidence provides one possibility; developing that evidence and the methodology for interpreting it was the heart of our work.

The writings of Hamilton and Madison are difficult to tell apart because both authors were masters of the popular *Spectator* style of writing—complicated and oratorical. To illustrate the difficulty, in 1941 Frederick Williams and Frederick Mosteller counted sentence lengths for the undisputed papers and got averages of 34.5 and 34.6 words respectively for Hamilton and Madison. For sentence length, a measure used successfully to distinguish other authors, Hamilton and Madison are practically twins.

MARKER WORDS

Although sentence length does measure complexity (and an average of 35 words shows that the material is very complex), sentence length is not sensitive enough to distinguish reliably between authors writing in similar styles. The variables used in several recent studies of disputed authorship are the rates of occurrence of specific individual words. Our study was stimulated by Adair's discovery—or rediscovery as it turned out—that Madison and Hamilton differ consistently in their choice between the alternative words *while* and *whilst*. In the 14 *Federalist* essays acknowledged to be written by Madison, *while* never occurs whereas *whilst* occurs in eight of them. *While* occurs in 15 of 48 Hamilton essays, but never a *whilst*. We have here an instance of what are called markers—items whose presence provides a strong indication of authorship for one of the men. Thus the presence of *whilst* in five of the disputed papers points toward Madison's authorship of those five.

Markers contribute a lot to discrimination when they can be found, but they also present difficulties. First, *while* or *whilst* occurs in less than half of the papers. They are absent from the other half, and hence give no evidence either way. We might hope to surmount this by finding enough different marker words or constructions so that one or more will always be present. A second and more serious difficulty is that from the evidence in 14 essays by Madison, we cannot be sure that he would never use *while*. Other writings of Madison were examined and, indeed, he did lapse on two occasions. The presence of *while* then is a good but not sure indication of Hamilton's authorship; the presence of *whilst* is a better, but still imperfect, indicator of Madison's authorship, for Hamilton too might lapse.

A central task of statistics is making inferences in the presence of uncertainty. Giving up the notion of perfect markers leads us to a statistical problem. We must find evidence, assess its strength, and combine it into a composite conclusion. Although the theoretical and practical problems may be difficult, the opportunity exists to assemble far more compelling evidence than even a few nearly perfect markers could provide.

RATES OF WORD USE

Instead of thinking of a word as a marker whose presence or absence settles the authorship of an essay, we can take the rate or relative frequency of use of each word as a measure pointing toward one or the other author. Of course, most words won't help because they were used at about the same rate by both authors. But since we have thousands of words available, some may help. Words form a huge pool of possible discriminators. From a systematic exploration of this pool of words, we found no more pairs like *while–whilst*, but we did find single words used by one author regularly but rarely by the other.

Table 1 shows the behavior of three words: *commonly, innovation, war*. The table summarizes data from 48 political essays known to be written by

TABLE 1. Frequency Distributions of Rate per 1000 Words in 48 Hamilton and 50 Madison Papers for *Commonly, Innovation*, and *War*

COMMONLY			INNOVATION			WAR		
Rate per 1000 Words	**H**	**M**	**Rate per 1000 Words**	**H**	**M**	**Rate per 1000 Words**	**H**	**M**
0 (exactly)*	31	49	0 (exactly)*	47	34	0 (exactly)*	23	15
0⁺–0.2	cannot occur†		0⁺–0.2	cannot occur†		0⁺–2	16	13
0.2–0.4	3	1	0.2–0.4		6	2– 4	4	5
0.4–0.6	6		0.4–0.6	1	6	4– 6	2	4
0.6–0.8	3		0.6–0.8		1	6– 8	1	3
0.8–1.0	2		0.8–1.0		2	8–10	1	3
1.0–1.2	2		1.0–1.2		1	10–12		3
1.2–1.4	1					12–14		2
						14–16	1	2
Totals	48	50	Totals	48	50	Totals	48	50

Source: Mosteller and Wallace (1964).
* Each interval, except 0 (exactly), excludes its upper end point. Thus a 2000-word paper in which *commonly* appears twice gives rise to a rate of 1.0 per 1000 exactly, and the paper appears in the count for the 1.0–1.2 interval.
† With the given lengths of the papers used, it accidentally happens that a rate in this interval cannot occur. For example, if a paper has 2000 words, a rate of 1 per 1000 means 2 words, and a single occurrence means a rate of 0.5 per 1000. Hence a 2000-word paper cannot lead to a rate per thousand greater than 0 and less than 0.5.

Hamilton and 50 known to be by Madison. (Some political essays from outside the *The Federalist,* but known to be by Hamilton or Madison, have been included in this study to give a broader base for the inference. Not all Hamilton's later *Federalist* papers have been included. We gathered more papers from outside *The Federalist* for Madison.)

Neither Hamilton nor Madison used *commonly* much, but Hamilton's use is much more frequent than Madison's. The table shows that in 31 of 48 Hamilton papers, the word *commonly* never occurred, but that in the other 17 it occurred one or more times. Madison used it only once in the 50 papers in our study. The papers vary in length from 900 to 3500 words, with 2000 about average. Even one occurrence in 900 words is a heavier usage than two occurrences in 3500 words, so instead of working with the number of occurrences in a paper, we use the rate of occurrence, with 1000 words as a convenient base. Thus, for example, the paper with the highest rate (1.33 per 1000 words) for *commonly* is a paper of 1500 words with 2 occurrences. *Innovation* behaves similarly, but it is a marker for Madison. For each of these two words, the highest rates are a little over 1 per 1000.

The word *war* has a spectacularly different behavior. Although absent from half of Hamilton's papers, when present it is used frequently—in one paper at a rate of 14 per 1000 words. *The Federalist* papers deal with specific topics in the Constitution and huge variations in the rates of such words as *war, law, executive, liberty,* and *trade* can be expected according to the context of the paper. Even though Madison uses *war* considerably more often then Hamilton in the undisputed papers, we explain this more by the division of tasks than by predilections of Madison for using *war.* Data from a word like *war* would give the same troublesome sort of evidence that historians have disagreed about over the last 100 years. Indeed, the dispute has continued because evidence from subject and content has been hopelessly inconclusive.

USE OF NON-CONTEXTUAL WORDS

For the statistical arguments to be valid, information from meaningful, contextual words must be largely discarded. Such a study of authorship will not then contribute directly to any understanding of the greatness of the papers, but the evidence of authorship can be both strengthened and made independent of evidence provided by historical analysis.

Avoidance of judgments about meaningfulness or importance is common in classification and identification procedures. When art critics try to authenticate a picture, in addition to the historical record, they consider little things: how fingernails and ears are painted, what kind of paint and canvas were used.

Relatively little of the final judgment is based upon the painting's artistic excellence. In the same way, police often identify people by their fingerprints, dental records, and scars, without reference to their personality, occupation, or position in society. For literary identification, we need not necessarily be clever about the appraisal of literary style, although it helps in some problems. To identify an object, we need not appreciate its full value or meaning.

What non-contextual words are' good candidates for discriminating between authors? Most attractive are the filler words of the language: prepositions, conjunctions, articles. Many other more meaningful words also seem relatively free from context: adverbs such as *commonly, consequently, particularly*, or even abstract nouns like *vigor* or *innovation*. We want words whose use is unrelated to the topic and may be regarded as reflecting minor or perhaps unconscious preferences of the author.

Consider what can be done with filler words. Some of these are the most used words in the language: *the, and, of, to,* and so on. No one writes without them, but we may find that their rates of use differ from author to author. Table 2 shows the distribution of rates for three prepositions—*by, from,* and *to*. First, note the variation from paper to paper. Madison uses *by* typically about 12 times per 1000 words, but sometimes has rates as high as 18 or as low as 6. Even on inspection though, the variation does not obscure

TABLE 2. Frequency Distribution of Rate per Thousand Words in 48 Hamilton and 50 Madison Papers for *By*, *From*, and *To*

BY			FROM			TO		
Rate per 1000 Words	H	M	Rate per 1000 Words	H	M	Rate per 1000 Words	H	M
1– 3*	2		1– 3*	3	3	20–25*		3
3– 5	7		3– 5	15	19	25–30	2	5
5– 7	12	5	5– 7	21	17	30–35	6	19
7– 9	18	7	7– 9	9	6	35–40	14	12
9–11	4	8	9–11		1	40–45	15	9
11–13	5	16	11–13		3	45–50	8	2
13–15		6	13–15		1	50–55	2	
15–17		5				55–60	1	
17–19		3						
Totals	48	50	Totals	48	50	Totals	48	50

Source: Mosteller and Wallace (1964).
* Each interval excludes its upper end point. Thus a paper with a rate of exactly 3 per 1000 words would appear in the count for the 3–5 interval.

Madison's systematic tendency to use *by* more often than Hamilton. Thus low rates for *by* suggest Hamilton's authorship, and high rates Madison's. Rates for *to* run in the opposite direction. Very high rates for *from* point to Madison but low rates give practically no information. The more widely the distributions are separated, the stronger the discriminating power of the word. Here, *by* discriminates better than *to,* which in turn is better than *from.*

PROBABILITY MODELS

To apply any of the theory of statistical inference to evidence from word rates, we must construct an acceptable probability model to represent the variability in word rate from paper to paper. Setting up a complete model for the occurrence of even a single word would be a hopeless task, for the fine structure within a sentence is determined in large measure by nonrandom elements of grammar, meaning, and style. But if our interest is restricted to the rates of use of one or more words in blocks of text of at least 100 or 200 words, we expect that detailed structure of phrases and sentences ought not to be very important. The simplest model can be described in the language of balls in an urn, so common in classical probability. To represent Madison's usage of the word *by,* we suppose there is a typical Madison rate, which would be somewhere near 12 per 1000, and we imagine an urn filled with many thousands of red and black balls, with the red occurring in the proportion 12 per 1000. Our probability model for the occurrence of *by* is the same as the probability model for successive draws from the urn, with a red ball corresponding to *by,* a black ball corresponding to all other words. To extend the model to simultaneous study of two or more words, we would need balls of three or more colors. No grammatical structure or meaning is a part of this model, and it is not intended to represent behavior within sentences. What is desired is that it explain the variation in rates— in counts of occurrences in long blocks of words, corresponding to the essays.

We tested the model by comparing its predictions with actual counts of word frequencies in the papers. We found that while this urn scheme reproduced variability well for many words, for other words additional variability was required. The random variation of the urn scheme represented most of the variation in counts from one essay to another, but in some essays authors change their basic rates a bit. We had to complicate the theoretical model to allow for this, and the model we used is called the negative binomial distribution.

The test showed also that pronouns like *his* and *her* are exceedingly unreliable authorship indicators, worse even than words like *war.*

INFERENCE AND RESULTS

Each possible route from construction of models to quantitative assessment of, say, Madison's authorship of some disputed paper, required solutions of serious theoretical statistical problems, and new mathematics had to be developed. A chief motivation for us was to use the *Federalist* problem as a case study for comparing several different statistical approaches, with special attention to one, called the Bayesian method, that expresses its final results in terms of probabilities, or odds, of authorship.

By whatever methods are used, the results are the same: overwhelming evidence for Madison's authorship of the disputed papers. For only one paper is the evidence more modest, and even there the most thorough study leads to odds of 80 to 1 in favor of Madison.

Figures 1 and 2 illustrate how the 12 disputed papers fit the distributions of Hamilton's and Madison's rates for two of the words finally chosen as discriminators. In Figure 1 the top two histograms portray the data for *by* that was given earlier in Table 2. Madison's rate runs higher on the average. Compare the bottom histogram for the disputed papers first with the top histogram for Hamilton papers, then with the second one for Madison papers. The rates in the disputed papers are, taken as a whole, very Madisonian, though 3 of the 12 papers by themselves are slightly on the Hamilton

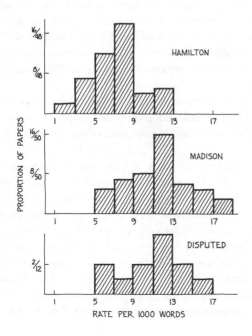

FIGURE 1

Distribution of rates of occurrence of by *in 48 Hamilton papers, 50 Madison papers, 12 disputed papers*

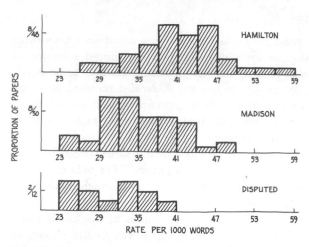

FIGURE 2

Distribution of rates of occurrence of to *in 48 Hamilton papers, 50 Madison papers, 12 disputed papers*

side of the typical rates.   Figure 2 shows the corresponding facts for *to*.   Here again the disputed papers are consistent with Madison's distribution, but further away from the Hamilton behavior than are the known Madison papers.

Table 3 shows the 30 words used in the final inference, along with the estimated mean rates per thousand in Hamilton's and Madison's writings. The groups are based upon the degree of contextuality anticipated by Mosteller and Wallace prior to the analysis.

The combined evidence from nine common filler words shown as group B was huge—much more important than the combined evidence from 20 low-frequency marker words like *while-whilst* and shown as groups C, D, and E.

There remains one word that showed up early as a powerful discriminator, sufficient almost by itself.   When should one write *upon* instead of *on?*   Even authoritative books on English usage don't provide good rules.   Hamilton and Madison differ tremendously.   Hamilton writes *on* and *upon* almost equally, about 3 times per 1000 words.   Madison, on the other hand, rarely uses *upon*.   Table 4 shows the distributions for *upon*.   In 48 papers Hamilton never failed to use *upon;* indeed, he never used it less than twice.   Madison only used it in 9 of 50 papers, and then only with low rates.   The disputed papers are clearly Madisonian with *upon* occurring in only one paper.   That paper, fortunately, is strongly classified by the other words.   It is not the paper with modest overall odds.

TABLE 3.   Words Used in Final Discrimination and Adjusted Rates of Use in Text by Madison and Hamilton

WORD	RATE PER 1000 WORDS		WORD	RATE PER 1000 WORDS	
	Hamilton	Madison		Hamilton	Madison
Group A			**Group D**		
Upon	3.24	0.23	Commonly	0.17	0.05
Group B			Consequently	0.10	0.42
Also	0.32	0.67	Considerable(ly)	0.37	0.17
An	5.95	4.58	According	0.17	0.54
By	7.32	11.43	Apt	0.27	0.08
Of	64.51	57.89	**Group E**		
On	3.38	7.75	Direction	0.17	0.08
There	3.20	1.33	Innovation(s)	0.06	0.15
This	7.77	6.00	Language	0.08	0.18
To	40.79	35.21	Vigor(ous)	0.18	0.08
Group C			Kind	0.69	0.17
Although	0.06	0.17	Matter(s)	0.36	0.09
Both	0.52	1.04	Particularly	0.15	0.37
Enough	0.25	0.10	Probability	0.27	0.09
While	0.21	0.07	Work(s)	0.13	0.27
Whilst	0.08	0.42			
Always	0.58	0.20			
Though	0.91	0.51			

Source: Mosteller and Wallace (1964).

Of course, combining and assessing the total evidence is a large statistical and computational task.   High speed computers were employed for many hours in making the calculations, both mathematical calculations for the theory, and empirical ones for the data.

You may have wondered about John Jay.   Might he not have taken a hand in the disputed papers?   Table 5 shows the rates per thousand for nine words of highest frequency in the English language measured in the writings of Hamilton, Madison, Jay, and, for a change of pace, in James Joyce's *Ulysses*.   The table supported the repeated assertion that Madison and Hamilton are similar.   Joyce is much different, but so is John Jay.   The words *of* and *to* with rate comparisons 65/58 and 41/35 were among the final discriminators between Hamilton and Madison.   See how much more easily Jay could be discriminated from either Hamilton or Madison by using *the, of, and, a,* and *that.*   The disputed papers are not at all consistent with Jay's rates, and there is no reason to question his omission from the dispute.

TABLE 4.   Frequency Distribution of Rate per Thousand Words in 48 Hamilton, 50 Madison, and 12 Disputed Papers for *Upon*

RATE PER 1000 WORDS	HAMILTON	MADISON	DISPUTED
0 (exactly)*		41	11
0+ –0.4		2	
0.4–0.8		4	
0.8–1.2	2	1	1
1.2–1.6	3	2	
1.6–2.0	6		
2.0–3.0	11		
3.0–4.0	11		
4.0–5.0	10		
5.0–6.0	3		
6.0–7.0	1		
7.0–8.0	1		
Totals	48	50	12

Source: Mosteller and Wallace (1964).
* Each interval, except 0 (exactly), excludes its upper endpoint.   Thus a paper with a rate of exactly 3 per 1000 words would appear in the count for the 3.0–4.0 interval.

TABLE 5.   Word Rates for High-Frequency Words
(Rates per 1000 Words)

	HAMILTON (94,000)*	MADISON (114,000)*	JAY (5000)*	JOYCE (ULYSSES) (260,000)*
The	91	94	67	57
Of	65	58	44	30
To	41	35	36	18
And	25	28	45	28
In	24	23	21	19
A	23	20	14	25
Be	20	16	19	3
That	15	14	20	12
It	14	13	17	9

Sources: Hanley (1937), Mosteller and Wallace (1964).
* The number of words of text counted to determine rates.

SUMMARY OF RESULTS

Our data independently supplement the evidence of the historians.   Madison is extremely likely, in the sense of degree of belief, to have written the disputed *Federalist* papers, with the possible exception of paper number 55, and there our evidence yields odds of 80 to 1 for Madison—strong, but not overwhelming.   Paper 56, next weakest, is a very strong 800 to 1 for Madison.   The data are overwhelming for all the rest, including the two papers historians feel weakest about, papers 62 and 63.

For a more extensive discussion of this problem, including historical details, discussion of actual techniques, and a variety of alternative analyses, see Mosteller and Wallace (1964).

PROBLEMS

1.   Why can't the authorship of the disputed papers be determined by literary style or political philosophy?

2.   (a) What is a discriminator?
     (b) Distinguish at least two categories of discriminators.
     (c) Why is *by* a good discriminator? (Refer to Table 2.)

3.   What is a "noncontextual word"?

4.   Why do the authors use word frequency per thousand words instead of just the number of occurrences?

5.   Refer to Table 1. In how many of the Hamilton papers studied does the word *commonly* appear at least once?

6.   Refer to Table 2. In what percentage of the Madison papers studied does *from* occur 3–7 times per 1000 words? (Note: The interval 3–7 uses the authors' convention on intervals.)

7.   Consider the "balls in an urn" model. How many colors of balls would we need to extend the model to the simultaneous study of 5 words? Of n words?

8.   Consider Figure 1. True or False: More than 1/3 of the Hamilton papers studied use *by* 3–7 times per 1000 words.

9.   Study Figure 2. Does the graph for the disputed papers look more like the graph for the Hamilton or the Madison papers?

10. Consider Table 3. Looking at group B, which word would you say was the best Hamilton/Madison discriminator? What was your word-selection criterion? Answer the same questions for group D.

11. Table 1 shows the relative frequency of *war*. Why doesn't *war* appear in Table 3?

REFERENCES

Miles L. Hanley. 1937. *Word Index to James Joyce's Ulysses.* Madison, Wis.: University of Wisconsin.

F. Mosteller and D. L. Wallace. 1964. *Inference and Disputed Authorship: The Federalist.* Reading, Mass.: Addison-Wesley.

POLICE MANPOWER VERSUS CRIME

S. James Press   *University of Chicago*

CRIME AND its prevention are much discussed these days, especially crimes of violence against individuals. Among the ways society moves to prevent or decrease crime, an important and time-honored one is the use of the police.

How effective are the police, and how may they be made more effective? For example, what impact does an increase of police manpower have? Such questions have in the past been remarkably little studied, in part because it is difficult and expensive to do the studies. This essay describes one study that was carried out where statistics played a central role. In this study, police manpower was increased substantially in one precinct of New York City. It was found that the manpower increase was accompanied by decreases in certain kinds of crime, in particular robbery and auto theft, but there were no changes in other kinds of crime, for example, burglary.

THE PROBLEM

To allocate police resources efficiently, it is useful to know whether the amount of crime committed in a given area is affected by increasing police manpower and associated equipment in the area; if crime is affected, by how much; and which crimes are affected the most. Getting at such questions requires careful statistical analysis because of a number of difficulties. Some difficulties are observational, in that data most appropriate for examining these questions have simply not been collected. Other difficulties are inherent in the problem. Some of them are:

(1) The true amount of crime committed in an area is never known precisely since only some fraction of it is actually reported. Further, the proportion reported may itself increase if police manpower increases.

(2) Crime changes must be analyzed in a controlled fashion so that the effects of changed. manpower can be compared with what crime *would* have been had the changes not been carried out. If crime patterns are continually shifting, such controlled study becomes more difficult. Thus, if an area experiences basic sociological or economic changes (such as might happen after an influx of low-income immigrants), patterns of crime might be expected to change independently of changes in police procedure.

(3) If a "crackdown on crime" is attempted in one area of the city and not in others, crime may decrease in that part of the city but increase in other parts as criminals merely relocate their activities. If such increases are spread over many areas in small amounts, their detection would be difficult because the effect would be masked by random fluctuations in reported crime, and by other factors external to the basic problem.

Because of data-gathering problems and inherent problems like those above, it has been difficult to quantify the effects of increased police manpower on crime. We shall see that statistical analysis helped clarify and interpret data from a New York City study in which police manpower was substantially increased in a single police precinct. Reported crimes in that precinct (and others) were recorded before and after the increase in police manpower.

The police made available data on daily reported crimes during the five-year period from January 1, 1963, to December 31, 1967. The crime reports were classified according to crime type (robbery, burglary, etc.), exact date, time, place, and nature of crime, and whether or not the crime was of the "outside" type (visible from the street). An example is shown by calendar quarter for "total robberies" in Figure 1.

On October 18, 1966, the police increased the number of patrolmen assigned to the 20th Precinct, located on the West Side of Manhattan (see

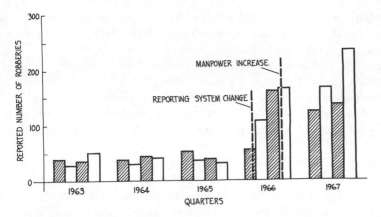

FIGURE 1
*Reported number of robberies
in the 20th Precinct. Source:
Press (1971)*

Figure 2), from an average of 212 to an average of 298 while police manpower elsewhere in the city remained fairly constant.

METHOD OF STUDY

The fundamental question of the study was whether the increase in police manpower decreased reported crimes. To answer this question, a number of analytic decisions had to be made, for example, should crimes be studied

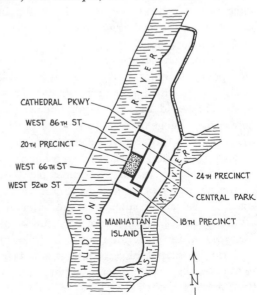

FIGURE 2
*Locations of police precincts
under study. Source: Press
(1971)*

on a daily, weekly, or some other time-period basis? The decision was to study crime on a weekly basis because of unevenness in the incidence of crime over the days of the week; more crime is committed on weekends.

A second analytic problem was that of seasonality; more outside crime is committed during the warmer months than during the colder months; for other crime types the reverse is true. A naive study of crime records might easily mistake an indicated increase for a "real" increase, rather than a seasonal effect. By using a statistical averaging technique this seasonal effect can be minimized.

The total period was divided into a low-manpower period (before the increase in police manpower) and a high-manpower period. The seasonally adjusted average weekly crime volumes during the low- and high-manpower periods could now be compared. Their differences, however, might not reflect the effect of increased police manpower since there was no control. That is, there was no way to tell whether an observed change in reported crime might have occurred anyhow—without a change in police manpower. To provide some measure of control for this effect (since it had not been provided by the design of the study), the following procedure was established. A group of precincts located in other parts of the city were selected as controls for the 20th Precinct, separately for each crime type, on the basis of how "similar" they were to the 20th, from a crime standpoint. Crime changes were then studied for the control precincts in the same way they were studied for the 20th Precinct. The difference in average weekly crime from low- to high-manpower periods in the 20th Precinct was compared with the average difference in the control precincts; the difference between these differences was taken to be the net effect associated with the increase in police manpower in the 20th Precinct.

The net changes in reported crime were evaluated as described above. At this point, decisions were made about which net changes were larger than could be explained by purely chance, or sampling variation. For example, if it were found that the estimated net change in reported crime (over and above the change in the control precincts) was a *decrease* of two crimes per week, was this observed change real, or just an effect explainable by purely chance (sampling) variation? Perhaps if the experiment were carried out again, a net *increase* of two crimes per week would be observed, just because of slightly different conditions at the times of observation. To reduce such uncertainties about interpretation, intervals of credibility, that is, intervals which reflect a high degree of belief in the net change results, were established. The idea behind these intervals is the following.

Prior to examining the data it was believed that almost any net change might be observed. After observing the data, however, it was determined (by means of statistical techniques) that uncertainty about the true net change of crime could then be confined to a rather small interval.

For example, suppose as in the illustration above, it were found that the observed net decrease in crime was about two crimes per week, and further, that the chance was very great (95%) that the *true* decrease was between 1.3 crimes per week and 2.6 crimes per week. Then, it could be concluded with little chance of error that a real decrease was being observed (since the interval includes only decreases) and that an observed increase would be highly unlikely in a future study. In many cases it was found that, although a net decrease or increase was observed, in fact, the interval of credibility included both positive and negative numbers and thus the apparent change could be attributable to sampling variation and might not be a real effect at all.

RESULTS

Some major results of the study are given in Table 1. A percentage change is relative to what would have occurred without the police manpower change. A net change was taken to be "statistically significant" if the 95% credibility interval included only positive or only negative numbers. In the table, all results are statistically significant unless the contrary is stated.

To understand how the numbers in the table were developed, consider the case of *outside robbery*. It was found that 4.56 crimes per week were reported on the average, in the 20th Precinct, prior to the substantial change

TABLE 1.   Changes in Crime Rate of Inside and Outside Crimes*

ROBBERY:	A net decrease of 2.6 crimes per week (33%) for crimes visible from the street and a net decrease of about 2 crimes per week (21%) for others
GRAND LARCENY:	A net decrease of 17 crimes per week (49%) for crimes visible from the street and a net decrease of 6.6 crimes per week (29%) for others
BURGLARY:	Changes in reported crime not visible from the street (97% of all burglaries in New York) were not statistically significant
AUTO THEFT:	There was a net decrease of 7.7 crimes per week (49%)
MISCELLANEOUS FELONIES:	There was a net decrease of 1.9 crimes per week (38%) for crimes visible from the street
TOTAL FELONIES:	A net decrease of 23.7 crimes per week (36%) for crimes visible from the street and a net decrease of 4.4 crimes per week (5%) for others
MISCELLANEOUS MISDEMEANORS:	Crimes visible from the street showed a net decrease of 8 crimes per week (15%); other crime changes were not statistically significant
TOTAL MISDEMEANORS:	Net changes were not statistically significant

* The data classified reported crimes as *outside crimes*, which are visible from the street, and *inside crimes*.

in police manpower (after adjustment for seasonal effects). After the manpower change, an average of 5.01 crimes per week were reported (after seasonal adjustment). In the control precinct, the corresponding numbers were 4.76 and 7.79, respectively. Thus, there was an increase of only 0.45 crimes per week in the 20th Precinct while there was an increase of 3.03 crimes per week in the control precinct (where there was *no* change in police manpower). The implication is that the reported number of outside robberies would have increased by 3.03 crimes per week (instead of only 0.45) during the same time interval had there not been a substantial increase in police manpower. The net effect of the police manpower change is 3.03 minus 0.45, or a decrease of about 2.6 crimes per week, the entry reported in the table. The 95% credibility interval was computed to be from 1.49 to 3.70. Since the interval included only decreases, it was concluded that the measured reduction in reported crime was a real effect.

It may be noted from the table that the increase in police manpower had little if any effect upon burglaries. This is not surprising since almost all burglaries are inside-type crimes. Placing more police in the neighborhood is not likely to have an appreciable effect upon such crimes unless the police manpower increase is accompanied by a change in the pattern of deployment to one which is designed to focus on burglaries.

The police manpower increase was accompanied by appreciable decreases in the violent crime of robbery (a crime that, by definition, requires a confrontation between criminal and victim) and the property crimes of grand larceny and auto theft. These results make sense since these crimes take place in the street, where a police manpower increase is likely to have its greatest effect.

TECHNICAL AND INTERPRETIVE PROBLEMS

Some of the technical difficulties which had to be overcome to arrive at the above conclusions, and some of the difficulties of interpretation of results of any such study, are described below.

Unfortunately, there was no opportunity for the statisticians to help in the design of the study so that, for example, the quality of the additional patrolmen (relative to the others) could not be assessed, the way in which the additional patrolmen were deployed and utilized could not be determined, and it could not be determined whether or not there was a *Hawthorne effect,* that is, a reduction or increase in reported crime simply because the patrolmen and residents knew a change was taking place (and therefore tried hard to effect a change). Also, the experiment was not repeated so that random errors would tend to average out. That is, several precincts in which police manpower was increased by the same percentage might have been, but were not, used. Another possibility might have been to increase police manpower (and then remove the additional force) several times in the 20th Precinct.

Moreover, the 20th Precinct might have peculiarities not common to the other precincts, and had several precincts been selected at random and the results averaged, results would have been more acceptable as representative of the City.

During the period of investigation the method of reporting crime underwent major changes. On March 10, 1966, a central reporting bureau was established for the entire city to replace the earlier precinct-by-precinct reporting system. Moreover, some of the definitions of what constitutes a reportable crime changed. The overall effect was to increase the number of reported crimes, that is, to reduce the number of crimes the police are aware of, but which previously may have gone unreported on official records. As a result, reported incidence of crime showed a substantial fictitious increase after the change in the reporting system. From an analysis standpoint, the data in the two periods (before and after the reporting system change) are not directly comparable so that reporting comparisons without statistical analysis would be misleading. (Data collected *after* the change in reporting system but *prior* to the increase in police manpower could be and were compared directly with data collected after the police manpower increase.) It was decided that although data collected before and after the reporting system change were somewhat different, the "early" data could at least be used to estimate the pattern of seasonal variation since that factor is likely to be least affected by changes in the reporting system. To evaluate seasonal variation, the early data were averaged in a special way designed to eliminate all effects except the seasonal component. Since the seasonal variation has a period of one year, the average was taken for one year periods over the approximately three years of data available prior to the change in reporting system. The results of this procedure were then used to eliminate the seasonal component from all the data collected subsequent to the change in reporting system.

It was also reasoned that when a new system of reporting crime is instituted it takes some time for the police personnel to adapt to the new system. That is, if crime records were used from the instant of adoption of the new system, part of any observed change in reported crime might be attributable to this transient effect. It was decided that about a month of adaptation time would be adequate, since over this period mistakes could be made one week, discovered during the next week or two, and corrected thereafter. After a month, most adaptation errors should have been eliminated.

In an analogous way, it was reasoned that after a substantial change in police manpower in an area the residents might change their rate of reporting crime, and therefore the reported incidence of crime. This might occur because of their increased awareness of the presence of police in the area, and therefore a greater feeling that something might be done about the crimes they report. To allow, at least in part, for the short-run aspect of this adaptation effect, the first month of data after the manpower increase began was not used in the detailed analysis.

SUMMARY

The problem of main interest was whether increased police manpower is effective as a deterrent to crime. In a New York City police precinct, police manpower was increased by 40%. Large volumes of data were collected for reported crime, over a five-year period, for all police precincts in the city. The simplest methods of summarizing the data could not, by themselves, be used to answer the question posed. By using techniques of seasonal adjustment, the method of comparison with control precincts, and credibility intervals, modern statistics was used to shed more light on a difficult problem. That is, by using statistical techniques, results were obtained, suggesting that, while increased police manpower is probably not very effective against certain types of crimes such as burglary and misdemeanors, it may be effective against other crimes such as robbery, grand larceny, and auto theft.

PROBLEMS

1. What is the common property or characteristic of the crimes against which an increase in police manpower seemed to be effective?

2. Does Figure 1 show that the 20th precinct had about 155 robberies in the third quarter of 1966? Explain your answer. (Hint: the answer is no.)

3. Figure 1 shows approximately 35 reported robberies in the second quarter of 1965 and 105 in the same quarter of 1966. Are these figures comparable? Explain.

4. If auto theft were the only crime under consideration, what seasonal variation, if any, would you expect?

5. Explain the system of control used in this study. Was it originally part of the design of the study? What is the weakness of this system of control?

6. What is an interval of credibility?

7. Consider the following table.

Changes in Crime Rate for Auto Theft

	20th Precinct	"Control" Precincts
Rate Before Manpower Increase	5.7/week	5.5/week
Rate After Manpower Increase	5.9/week	6.7/week

(a) What is the estimated net effect of the manpower increase on the auto theft rate in the 20th precinct?

(b) If the interval of credibility were −1.2 to .5 crimes per week with 95% credibility would we conclude we had a true change?

(c) If the interval of credibility were −1.2 to −.5 crimes per week with 95% credibility would we conclude we had a true change?

Explain your answers.

8. Consider Table 1 (and the accompanying text). Which crime(s) showed "statistically significant" changes?

9. What is the meaning of the term *Hawthorne effect*?

10. How did the study's analysis take account of the change in the system of reporting crimes?

REFERENCES

A. D. Biderman. 1967. "Surveys of Population Samples for Estimating Crime Incidence." *The Annals of the American Academy of Political and Social Science* 374: Nov.

"The Challenge of Crime in a Free Society." *A Report by the President's Commission on Law Enforcement and the Administration of Justice.* Washington: U.S. Government Printing Office. Feb. 1967.

"Criminal Victimization in the United States: A Report of a National Survey." *Field Survey II,* The President's Commission on Law Enforcement and the Administration of Justice, National Opinion Research Center, Chicago. May 1967.

"Operation 25." 1955. City of New York Police Department.

S. J. Press. 1971. "Some Effects of an Increase in Police Manpower in the 20th Precinct of New York City." R-704-NYC. New York: The New York City RAND Institute.

VARIETIES OF MILITARY LEADERSHIP

Hanan C. Selvin   *State University of New York, Stony Brook*

WORKERS ON an assembly line, students in a third-grade classroom, and soldiers in an army training camp do different kinds of work in radically different settings, but they have in common one important social relationship. They all spend a good part of their day in close contact with lower-level leaders, such as foremen, teachers, and company-level officers, both commissioned and noncommissioned. From both individual experience and empirical research we know that the behavior of workers, students, soldiers, and others in subordinate positions, at work and afterward, is significantly affected by the actions of their leaders.

The empirical study reported here shows how the actions of company leaders in twelve U.S. Army training companies affected the *nonduty* behavior of several hundred soldiers undergoing basic training. The unraveling of these effects of leadership was unusually complex. Unlike the student and the worker, who usually are subject to only one leader in the course of a working day, the trainee had two company-level commissioned officers (the Commanding Officer and the Executive Officer) and two company-level "non-coms" (the First Sergeant and the Field First Sergeant). There was constant turnover in these positions: during his training cycle the typical trainee had seven company-level leaders.

An additional source of complexity in this study is the way in which we constructed descriptions of the "leadership climates" of the companies. For this study, it seemed better to rely on the trainees' description of their leaders in a questionnaire that they filled out at the end of their basic training, rather than on judgments by superiors or outside experts, as is often done in evaluating how well an organization achieves its goals. Accordingly, each trainee rated each of his leaders on fifteen different questions, ranging from how well the leader inspired confidence to whether he punished the men at every opportunity.

The sheer bulk of these data is impressive: an average of 150 men in each of 12 companies rated an average of 7 leaders on 15 questions. Multiplying these figures together ($150 \times 12 \times 7 \times 15$) yields a total of about 189,000 separate ratings of company leaders. The major statistical problem was to boil down this mass of data into descriptions of the leadership climates of the companies.

Part of this statistical "boiling down," or *data reduction* as it is usually called, consisted of such simple procedures as computing averages. Another large part, much more complex and more illuminating, was a statistical procedure called *factor analysis,* which played a central part in measuring the leadership climates. These factor-analytic procedures not only exemplify a powerful technique, but also can be applied whenever several people can give independent judgments about someone with whose behavior they are familiar. Examples are teachers as described by their students, students as described by several teachers, and mental hospital patients as seen by the ward staff. Finally, although most studies of teaching effectiveness in colleges and universities rely on ratings of the teachers by their students, they do not typically go on to the kind of analytic clarification that this procedure would afford.

THE IDEA OF FACTOR ANALYSIS

The three primary colors (red, yellow, and blue) when suitably combined, yield thousands of different colors. Similarly every bit of matter can be analyzed into some combination of the hundred-odd chemical elements. These two facts, familiar to all adults from their school days, are parallels in the realm of physical science to what the statistical procedure of factor analysis can sometimes do with such social phenomena as opinions, votes, and symptoms of mental illness. Factor analysis is, in short, a way to discover or construct from a larger group of observed characteristics, or *items,* a small set of more general characteristics, or *factors,* various combinations of which will produce each of the observed patterns of items.

THE BACKGROUND FOR THE DATA

To explain this work, let us start with the gathering of the data at Fort Dix, New Jersey, in the spring of 1952 by two physicians, Arthur M. Arkin and Thomas M. Gellert, then on the staff of the Mental Health Consultation Service (a central psychiatric facility to which soldiers were referred from dispensaries located near their companies). Over a period of several months they began to notice patterns in their records. Some companies had higher rates of accidents, other companies suffered more psychosomatic illnesses, and still other companies had greater proportions of men going AWOL for short periods. Because all companies followed essentially the same program of training, lived in identical barracks, and ate the same food, the staff members speculated about the kinds of factors that might be responsible for the differences they had observed. They reasoned that differences in the nature of the leadership among companies might account for the differences in rates of accidents, of psychosomatic illnesses, and of going AWOL.

Further reflections and some pilot studies soon led to the development of the two questionnaires that are the basis of this study. One, the "behavior questionnaire," asked each trainee to report the frequency of 24 kinds of nonduty behavior, such as going to the PX for food between meals, having sexual intercourse, going to the movies, and seeing the Chaplain. This questionnaire also asked for the trainee's age, education, and marital status.

The second questionnaire dealt with the company-level leaders that the trainee had had during the sixteen weeks of basic training: Commanding Officer (C.O.), Executive Officer (Exec.), First Sergeant (1/Sgt.) and Field First Sergeant (F-1/Sgt.). In general, the C.O. and the F-1/Sgt. worked directly with the trainees, and the other two leaders usually remained in the company office, or orderly room, and had less contact with the men.

APPROACHES TO THE ANALYSIS

Three elements combined to shape the analysis of the leadership data: the nature of the data as described above, the properties of the available statistical methods, and my training as a sociologist. At the outset of the analysis, there was a choice between two essentially different problems: the *psychological* problem of trying to explain a particular event (say, why Pvt. John Doe got drunk on his first weekend pass) and the *sociological* problem of variations in *rates* of behavior in different social units (why, for example, did Doe's company have a higher proportion of men getting drunk than did any other company?).

I chose to work on the second problem, both because of my training as a sociologist and because the data lacked the detailed psychological information on each individual soldier needed to learn why he behaved as he did. Once made, this decision helped to shape the answer to the second basic question of the study: how to describe the leadership of each company. It gradually became clear to my assistant (E. David Nasatir) and me that the data had to be put together in two different ways. First, we wanted to describe the leadership behavior of all of the leaders in a company, not simply that of the C.O.; we expected the nonduty behavior of the trainees to be affected by the overall leadership climate of the company. (We were able to show that each leader contributed something of his own to that climate and that his actions were not simply copies of the actions of the C.O.) Second, all of the leadership data we had were embodied in the responses of the individual trainees, so it was necessary to combine the responses in some way for two reasons. We wanted to find the common elements in the evaluations of leadership in a company, not the idiosyncratic perceptions of one or a few trainees, and, consistent with our sociological orientation, we wanted to focus on how the trainees in each company, as a group, saw their leaders.

The central statistical task is thus to describe the entire set of company-level leaders as seen by the entire set of trainees in each company, in other words, to reduce the 189,000 ratings of the 82 leaders by the 1800 trainees on the 15 questions to a small set of descriptions of each company's leadership climate.

THE IDEAL STUDY AND THE REAL STUDY

It will clarify the statistical reasoning to put the questionnaires aside for a moment and ask how one would go about describing leadership climates if one had unlimited resources of money, trained personnel, and time.

Ideally, perhaps, one would assemble a group of trained observers—or even one "omniscient observer"—and ask them to live with each company for a significant part of its training cycle. These observers would watch, record, and evaluate the behavior of the leaders and somehow produce a concise description of each company's leadership climate.

Even if everything were ideal, this would be extraordinarily difficult. For one thing, the observers would have to be everywhere, watching everything, and yet not interfering with the training activities or affecting the nature of the leadership. No, a corps of observers would not do, but if we could depart altogether from a realistic observational situation, at least to the extent of thinking of what an ideal arrangement might be, we would like to have an omniscient observer, a kind of observational superman who could see every interaction, describe it, and combine it appropriately with all of the thousands

TABLE 1.   How Pvt. Doe Answered Question 15 of Leadership Questionnaire

	C.O.	Exec. Off.	1st Sgt.	Field 1/Sgt.
15. If you were ordered into combat and you could choose the men who would be your leaders use the No. 1 for those men in your unit you would like MOST to lead you; No. 2 for those men whom you would like LESS to lead you; and the No. 3 for those men you would like LEAST to lead you if at all.	*1* *3*	*2*	*2* *1*	*3* *3*

of others that he observes.   Such an omniscient observer does not exist, but we were able to create an approximation to his observations statistically by basing the descriptions of the leaders' behavior on the experience of the trainees.   To see how this was done, consider question 15 (see Table 1) of the leadership questionnaire filled out by Pvt. John Doe of company X.

During his 16 weeks of training, Doe had seven company-level leaders: two C.O.'s, one Executive Officer, two First Sergeants, and two Field First Sergeants.   The numbers at the right in Table 1 are his ratings of each officer and noncom as a combat leader.   Doe apparently thought that the first C.O. would have made a good combat leader, for he gave him the hightest rating, 1.   His unwillingness to follow the second C.O. into combat is indicated by the low rating of 3.

Every trainee in Doe's company rated the same company-level officers on this question.   For the sake of illustration, assume that there were 100 trainees in this company and that their ratings of the first C.O. as a combat leader were those shown in Table 2.   The average of these ratings is 1.70, so this is the rating that the first C.O. was assigned on combat leadership.

TABLE 2.   Ratings Given to First C.O. by 100 Trainees

RATING (1)	NUMBER OF TRAINEES (2)	(1) × (2)
1	50	50
2	30	60
3	20	60
	100	170

$$\text{Average} = \frac{170}{100} = 1.70$$

We can now turn away from the trainees and take each average rating as a characteristic of the leader being rated. Thus the first C.O. in the illustrative example would be said to have a rating of 1.70 as a combat leader. In other words, the average ratings received by a leader may be considered as his (*perceived*) attributes.

In the leadership questionnaire each leader was rated, as in the foregoing illustration, on the extent that he:

(1) Influenced the lives of the trainees
(2) Commanded the respect of the trainees
(3) Was a "sucker for sob stories"
(4) Was a "good Joe" one minute and "mean as Hell" the next
(5) Could create a real fighting spirit against the enemy
(6) Acted in such a way that the trainees were afraid of him
(7) Could not be depended on to keep his promises
(8) Created a feeling of confidence in the trainees
(9) Told the trainees when he thought that an order from higher headquarters was unfair or silly
(10) Displayed a real interest in the trainees without babying them
(11) Treated the trainees "like dirt"
(12) Gave more breaks to his favorite trainees than to others
(13) Seized every opportunity to punish his men
(14) Tried to have his men excused from "dirty details" ordered by higher authorities
(15) Would be preferred as a leader in combat

This use of average ratings, instead of the original ratings by each of the trainees, yields an impressive reduction in the amount of data. Instead of some 189,000 individual ratings, there are now only 1230 averages (82 leaders rated on 15 questions). Even more important than the quantity, however, is the quality of these statistically derived data. The original ratings of each leader show a great deal of variation, with misperception, failure to follow instructions, facetiousness, and errors of processing all distorting the true ratings.

COVARIATION OF RATINGS

The quality of these average ratings appears most clearly when we see how much the characteristics of the leaders that *should* vary together *do* vary together. To show this, we must introduce a numerical measure of this joint variation. We chose the *coefficient of correlation,* invented by Sir Francis Galton in the 1880s to measure how much various physical characteristics, such as height, are inherited. If the height of a son can be predicted *exactly* by a mathematical equation for a straight line using the height of his father and if tall fathers give rise to tall sons, then the value of the correlation coefficient is 1.0, the largest value that this coefficient can have. If the height of a son can be predicted exactly from the height of his father, but tall fathers produce short sons, then the value of the correlation coefficient is —1.0, its largest negative value. And, if there were no relation between the heights of fathers and the heights of sons, the correlation coefficient would be 0. (See the essay by Whitney for a further description of the correlation coefficient.)

In real data on individuals, values close to 1.0 or —1.0 are rare. Thus the correlations between pairs of ratings given to any one leader by the men in his company seldom were higher than 0.30. These are, of course, the correlations between the responses of the individual trainees to the leadership questions, before the computation of averages. For example, a trainee who rated a particular leader high as a combat leader might be almost as likely to rate him low in displaying an interest in the trainees as he would be to rate him high on this second trait.

The situation is altogether different for the average ratings. For example, a leader who has a high average rating on instilling a fighting spirit in his men (question 5) almost always has a high average rating on commanding their respect (question 2); the correlation between the averages on these two characteristics is 0.82. Similarly, a leader who punishes at every opportunity (question 13) usually produces fear (question 6); the correlation in this case is 0.84. The size of these correlations between averages is striking: of the 105 correlations in the leadership data, 49 are numerically greater than 0.50, 28 are numerically greater than 0.70, and 13 are numerically greater than 0.80.

On the other hand, we might expect competence and coercion to be negatively related—that, by and large, leaders who were judged to be competent would be less likely to be judged coercive. The data only partially bear out this expectation. The correlations between the average scores on inspiring respect and the averages on the two questions that measure coerciveness (6 and 13) are moderately negative (—0.28 for the question on fear and —0.45 for the one on punishment), but the corresponding correlations between the averages on the question on instilling a fighting spirit and the averages on the measures of coerciveness are so close to zero (—0.01 and —0.16) that they indicate that there is no appreciable relation.

Even though there are only four items in the analysis in the previous paragraph, the discussion was a bit complicated. Part of this complexity might be removed by a better choice of words, but there is a limit to the complexity that words can clarify. Imagine the complexity in trying to relate all 105 correlation coefficients between pairs of averages, instead of only four!

USING FACTOR ANALYSIS TO DESCRIBE THE STRUCTURE OF LEADERSHIP

Factor analysis offers a way out of this complexity. This statistical procedure often makes it possible to untangle large sets of correlation coefficients; in brief it determines which items go together and which do not. Moreover, it expresses this structure of relations numerically, so that we can tell *how much* of what kinds of order there is in the set of correlations and how these simpler orders fit together.

Before turning to the leadership data it is important to say a few words about the goals of factor analysis. In psychology, the field where factor analysis was invented and has been most used, it is customary to speak of the statistically derived factors as "underlying," "basic," or "fundamental" variables and to use the verbs "discover" or "uncover" to describe the process used to calculate the factors. This language suggests that psychologists and statisticians have invented a statistical procedure for discovering scientific truths, much as chemists discovered the 100-odd fundamental chemical elements. I prefer to use a different set of terms. I shall speak of "constructing new variables," or factors, from combinations of the original items. The statistical procedures are the same; only the shades of meaning attached to them differ.

It turns out that the 15 original questions in the leadership data can be combined into 3 new variables or factors, which we labeled "positive leadership," "tyrannical leadership," and "vacillating leadership." For example, a leader who received averages close to 1 on the question of willingness to follow into combat and on similar questions that make up the factor of positive leadership would get a high score on that factor. The factor-analytic computations thus lead to a set of scores for each leader on the 3 factors, scores that, to a considerable extent, can replace his scores on the 15 original variables. That is, if we know a leader's scores on these factors, then we can estimate his average ratings for the 15 original questions with a high degree of accuracy. The statistical relations between items and factors suggest the names for the factors. Thus a leader who scores high on the factor of positive leadership is one who creates confidence in the trainees, is able to instill a fighting spirit in his men, is interested in them, and is one whom the men would like to have leading them in combat. Similarly, leaders who receive high scores on the second factor, tyrannical leadership, are likely to be seen as producing fear in the trainees, as punishing them at every opportunity, and as treating them "like dirt." High scores on vacillating leadership go to leaders who play favorites, punish at every opportunity, and are "Good Joes one minute and mean as Hell the next."

The construction of the 3 factors from the original 15 items was entirely a statistical operation, based only on the numerical correlations among the 15 items. Neither the wording of the questions nor the analyst's expectations entered into these computations. These nonstatistical considerations enter only in choosing the names for the factors, and even these choices are relatively unimportant when one has access to all the significant numerical results.

VERIFYING THE MEANING OF THE FACTORS

Instead of dreary columns of numbers, let us look at other, perhaps more meaningful evidence that these factors really do express the trainees' perceptions of their leaders. The evidence comes from the unsolicited comments that many trainees wrote on the leadership questionnaires. For example, one trainee wrote of an officer who turned out to have a particularly high positive-leadership score:

> I think that our commanding officer, Capt. ————, was a great leader, he held the respect of all the men and was just about everyone's choice to lead them in combat if we ever saw action.

And a First Sergeant who happened to receive a conspicuously low score on this dimension elicited the remark:

> . . . he is the most unsympathetic character that I have ever encountered in my life also sneaky . . . . I don't see how he ever earned his stripes for he has the mental capabilities of a mongoloid.

Similarly, an officer with a very high score on tyrannical leadership drew this comment:

> The C.O. beat men until they ran to the I.G. (Inspector General). Very few of us got passes during basic. We never got breaks in our marches because the C.O. was either trying to set a record or win some money.

Finally, of the leader who had the highest score on the factor of vacillating leadership, one trainee wrote:

> If [he] wouldn't lie to the men so much and stop trying to make major . . . this soldier hates his guts for the way he treated me and the rest in basic training.

The last quotation may seem almost as indicative of tyrannical as of vacillating leadership. Indeed, we shall shortly see that there was a high correlation between these two factors.

LEADERSHIP CLIMATE OF COMPANIES

The computation of factor scores simplifies the data a good deal; instead of there being, for each of 82 leaders, scores on 15 items, there are only the scores on the 3 factors. One more important step remains: to combine the scores for each leader in a company into measures of the *leadership climate* of that company. At first glance it might appear that one could take a simple average of the leadership factor scores for the leaders in each company. There are two reasons, however, for not doing this. First, the leaders did not all serve the same length of time; some were with their companies for the entire 16 weeks, but others served as little as 2 weeks of the training cycle. Second, the leaders also varied in the extent of their influence on the trainees. In general, C.O.'s and Field First Sergeants had more influence than did leaders in the other two positions. And, of course, the personal qualities of the leaders also made some of them more significant than others.

Fortunately, one of the questions on the leadership questionnaire made it possible to measure the relative influence of the leaders:

> (1) The four men listed on the right side of this paper are all important in the life of a trainee. Place the No. 1 in the column under the name or names of the men who had the MOST influence in your life as a trainee; the No. 2 in the column under the name or names of the men who had LESS influence and the No. 3 in the column under the name or names of the men who had the LEAST influence or NONE AT ALL.

The average score received by each leader on this question can serve as a measure of his perceived relative importance in determining the leadership climate of his company. Incidentally, the Field First Sergeant had the most influence just as often as the C.O., thus bearing out the point made earlier, that there is more to the effects of leadership than rank alone.

It seems obvious that the dimensions of leadership climate should be the same as the three factors of leader behavior, provided that the scores on these factors can be modified to take into account the variations in length of service and in importance to the trainees. A procedure for doing this uses a modified, or *weighted*, average; each leader's factor scores are given more or less weight according to his length of service and his relative importance. Thus, in the "indexes of leadership climate" for the company, a leader who served all 16 weeks would have his factor scores counted twice as heavily as a leader who served only 8 weeks. Similarly, leaders with high "influence scores" would have their three factor scores weighted more heavily in the indexes of leadership climate than would leaders with low "influence scores."

Computing these weighted averages of the factor scores yields three indexes of leadership climate for each company, one for each factor of leadership. For this study, it suffices to condense these indexes into only two values, "high" and "low" (actually, relatively high and relatively low). A further simplification comes from the high correlation between the indexes of tyranny and vacillation. With only one exception, companies high on tyranny were also high on vacillation. With only 12 companies, it was impossible to separate tyranny from vacillation.

TABLE 3.   Types of Leadership Climate

INDEXES OF LEADERSHIP		LEADERSHIP CLIMATES	NUMBER OF COMPANIES
Positive	Tyrannical and Vacillating		
High	High	Paternal	1
High	Low	Persuasive	6
Low	High	Arbitrary	3
Low	Low	Weak	2
		Total	12

When this is done, there are only four different types of leadership climate, corresponding to high and low values on the first two indexes of leadership climate, as shown in Table 3.

The statistical techniques of averaging, correlation, and factor analysis have made it possible to distill these four types of leadership climate from the 189,000 separate ratings of leaders.   Simply in the sense of reducing a mass of virtually indigestible data to a set of straightforward types, this is impressive.   Data reduction alone was not the point of this research; rather, it was to study the effect of leadership on nonduty behavior.   The value of this statistical analysis thus lies in finding how much difference these types of leadership climate make in the patterns of nonduty behavior.   The gross differences in rates of different kinds of behavior between leadership climates are seldom larger than 10 percentage points, but they are remarkably consistent. There is space here only to sketch these effects; for further details the reader may consult Selvin (1960, especially Chapters 5 to 7).

EFFECTS OF LEADERSHIP ON BEHAVIOR

Because of a change in the behavior questionnaire during the gathering of the data, it was not possible to compare the frequencies of different kinds of nonduty behavior in the "paternal" climate with the rates in the other three climates.   The remaining three climates—"persuasive," "weak," and "arbitrary"—can be thought of as spanning the continuum from competent, democratic, and considerate leadership to incompetent, coercive, and unsympathetic leadership.   By and large, these differences in type of leadership correspond to the differences in frequencies and patterns of nonduty activities. The "persuasive" climate has the lowest rates on many of the nonduty activities, the "weak" has intermediate levels, and the "arbitrary" has the highest; or, to put it quantitatively, comparing the rates in the three climates with the rates for all trainees taken together, the rates in the "arbitrary" climate

TABLE 4. Proportion Reporting Getting Drunk at Least Once During Basic Training, by Leadership Climate

"Persuasive" climate	25%
"Weak" climate	36%
"Arbitrary" climate	34%

are higher than the rates for all trainees in 13 activities, the rates in the "weak" climate are higher in 9 and the rates in the "persuasive" climate are higher in 5 activities.

As an illustration of the type of relation found in this study, consider the effect of leadership climate on the incidence of drunkenness. In answer to the question "How many times during basic training did you get really drunk?" the figures shown in Table 4 were obtained. The maximum difference in this table, 11 percentage points between "persuasive" and "weak" climates, is typical of most of the differences between leadership climates in this study. They were usually no larger than 10 percentage points. This may not seem like much of a difference. Does the smallness of this relation mean that leadership has little effect on nonduty activities? Or does leadership have a larger effect, one that somehow does not appear in these figures?

The latter conjecture seems to be correct. The effects of leadership differences bear unequally on different kinds of men, some showing great differences in their rates of specific nonduty activities from one leadership climate to another and others seeming almost immune to differences in leadership. Thus consider the same relation between leadership and drunkenness, but this time examined separately for single and married men (see Table 5).

Compare the two columns with each other and with the figures in the preceding table. Among the single men, leadership climate has only a small effect on rates of drunkenness; the difference between the highest and lowest is only

TABLE 5. Proportion Reporting Getting Drunk at Least Once During Basic Training, by Leadership Climate and Marital Status

	SINGLE MEN	MARRIED MEN
"Persuasive" climate	30%	14%
"Weak" climate	38%	32%
"Arbitrary" climate	33%	36%

8 percentage points. Among the married men the picture is altogether different. The difference between the highest and lowest rates is 22 percentage points, almost three times as much.

Similar findings hold for most of the activities in this study and for the other two individual characteristics on which data were gathered, age and education. The effects of leadership are felt most among the older, married trainees who had not graduated from high school, and they are felt least among the younger, single high-school graduates. Statisticians express relations like these by saying that the leadership climate and individual characteristics *interact* in their effects on behavior; the effects of leadership climate on behavior depend on the background of the trainee, and, correspondingly, the effects of background on behavior vary from one kind of leadership climate to another. In short, the types of leadership climate constructed by the elaborate statistical procedure described in this chapter not only make sense; they also make a difference.

OTHER APPLICATIONS OF STATISTICS IN EVALUATING INDIVIDUALS

The method of describing leadership climate by a combination of statistical procedures appears to be applicable to a wide range of situations in which an individual (a leader, a doctor, a patient, or even an inanimate object like a book, picture, musical performance, or other aesthetic object) is rated independently on a number of variables by a group of judges, each of whom is well acquainted with the individuals he is rating. Perhaps the most significant extension of this work would be its application to other kinds of military units, both in training and in combat. Such studies should also examine what this study chose to ignore, the effects of leadership on the performance of assigned duties as well as nonduty behavior.

PROBLEMS

Note: Table 1 is incomplete.

1. The object of this study was to make some statement about off-duty behavior of enlisted men. Why did the author feel it was important to determine leadership climate?

2. Explain the idea of factor analysis.

3. The author draws a distinction between a *psychological* and *sociological* problem. Explain this distinction.

4. At what stage in the data reduction were the coefficients of correlation obtained?

5. Consider the author's statement: "Imagine the complexity in trying to relate all 105 correlation coefficients between pairs of averages, instead of only four!" Why are there 105 such correlation coefficients? (Hint: There are 15 questions.)

6. What would be the meaning of a correlation of −.77 between two questions? A correlation of .15?

7. Suppose the author had relied on his prior expectations of correlation to determine the three factors. How would this affect the nature of the study? Would it necessarily affect the outcome of the study?

8. In Table 3, why are "tyrannical" and "vacillating" combined into one category?

9. How were the terms "paternal", "persuasive", "arbitrary", and "weak" chosen to describe the various leadership climates?

10. Which leadership climate tended to have associated the most desirable off-duty behavior?

11. Consider Table 5. True or false: For each leadership climate, a greater percentage of single than married men reported getting drunk at least once. Explain your answer.

12. What does a statistician mean by the term *interact*?

REFERENCES

Raymond Bernard Cattell. 1952. *Factor Analysis: An Introduction and Manual for the Psychologist and Social Scientist.* New York: Harper. Probably the clearest account of the principles of factor analysis.

Harry H. Harman. 1960. *Modern Factor Analysis.* Chicago: University of Chicago. This is a very technical, but encyclopedic, book.

Hanan C. Selvin. 1960. *The Effects of Leadership.* New York: Free Press.

REGISTRATION AND VOTING

Edward R. Tufte   *Princeton University*

THE QUESTIONS

If citizens are to express their preferences on election day in the U.S., they must register to vote some weeks or even months prior to the election. The inability or failure to do so deprives the citizens of their votes. Many other democracies have automatic registration of all voters or no registration procedures at all. What are the consequences, if any, of the more elaborate voter registration practices in the U.S.? And furthermore, since the particular rules for registration differ greatly from place to place throughout the country, what are the consequences of such differences?

Recently several students of politics sought to answer these questions by analyzing quantitative data on registration and voting. In particular, they discovered answers to questions such as "Why does the proportion of citizens registered to vote differ so much in different cities? Why are, for example, 96% of all eligible citizens registered in South Bend, Indiana, about 65% in New York City and Dallas, and only 34% in Atlanta? Why is voter

114

turnout on election day in the U.S. lower than in other democracies, such as England, France, Norway, and Canada?"

Many have suggested answers to these questions. For example, some have felt that the low voter turnout in the U.S. occurs because American citizens are more apathetic than their counterparts in other democracies. But when this suggestion and others are investigated more precisely and deeply with careful statistical procedures, not all of the old speculations prove to be correct. And the new answers have important consequences for increasing political participation in the U.S.

THE IDEAS BEHIND THE STUDY OF REGISTRATION AND VOTING

A key part of the idea of democracy is that citizens participate in the choice of their leaders. Constraints on the ability of citizens to participate in politics restrict voting to those who have the resources and energy to overcome such obstacles. In theory, citizens will generally make greater efforts to overcome limitations on their ability to participate if they feel their efforts will amount to something; that is, if a citizen feels his vote will make a difference, he may be willing to stand in line to register weeks before the election and then, on election day, walk through the rain in order to cast a ballot. This reasoning, which suggests that people assess (whether consciously or unconsciously) the costs and potential benefits of registering and voting, implies that citizens will be more likely to register and then later vote if the costs of registering to vote are low and the election is thought to be closely contested. In other words, citizens may attach more value to their votes, and therefore be more likely to vote, if they think the election is going to be close simply because they believe their votes might make a difference, other things being equal. Now it is important to note at this point that these assertions have not been proven; they are only a plausible theory. Three scholars at Princeton University—Stanley Kelley, Jr., Richard E. Ayres, and William G. Bowen—set out to test these ideas. Let us now see what they learned about registration and voting in their study.

THE STUDY AND THE RESULTS

Their first question was "Do rates of registration vary in different parts of the country and, if so, are the differences in registration rates important in a political sense?" In studying 104 of the nation's largest cities, they found that voter registration rates ranged from a high of 96.4% of those of voting age who were registered in South Bend, Indiana, to a low of 32.1% in Columbus, Georgia.

Table 1 shows both the registration and the voting rates for all 104 cities. The rates varied a great deal from city to city and, moreover, registration

TABLE 1.   Registration and Voting Rates in 104 Cities, 1960*

CITY	REGISTRATION RATE AS PERCENT OF VOTING AGE POPULATION	TURNOUT RATE AS PERCENT OF VOTING AGE POPULATION
South Bend, Ind.	96.4	85.2
Des Moines, Iowa	92.6	71.6
Minneapolis, Minn.	92.5	58.5
Detroit, Mich.	92.0	70.0
Seattle, Wash.	92.0	70.8
Lansing, Mich.	91.9	72.4
St. Paul, Minn.	91.2	72.1
Berkeley, Calif.	90.5	70.4
Scranton, Pa.	90.4	80.3
Spokane, Wash.	89.4	67.0
Dearborn, Mich.	89.3	81.2
Albany, N. Y.	88.4	87.2
Torrance, Calif.	87.7	76.5
Peoria, Ill.	87.4	64.9
Gary, Ind.	87.3	72.5
Tacoma, Wash.	87.3	67.8
Salt Lake City, Utah	87.0	76.6
Portland, Ore.	85.8	74.1
Duluth, Minn.	85.1	74.9
Glendale, Calif.	84.9	73.1
Memphis, Tenn.	84.7	50 1
Hammond, Ind.	84.0	71.3
Pasadena, Calif.	83.2	69.2
Grand Rapids, Mich.	83.2	72.9
Buffalo, N. Y.	83.0	69.7
New Bedford, Mass.	82.4	74.6
Tulsa, Okla.	82.4	69.4
Rockford, Ill.	82.0	75.1
Topeka, Kans.	81.9	69.3
Fort Wayne, Ind.	81.7	71.1
Waterbury, Conn.	81.4	77.4
Camden, N. J.	81.3	69.0
Pittsburgh, Pa.	81.2	68.3
Fresno, Calif.	81.1	44.6
Jersey City, N. J.	81.1	72.8
Worcester, Mass.	81.0	74.0
Youngstown, Ohio	81.0	71.6
Canton, Ohio	80.9	73.2
Oklahoma City, Okla.	80.4	62.7
Omaha, Neb.	79.8	66.8
Flint, Mich.	79.6	69.4
Lincoln, Neb.	79.4	64.5
Cincinnati, Ohio	79.4	67.9

TABLE 1.   Registration and Voting Rates in 104 Cities, 1960* (*Continued*)

CITY	REGISTRATION RATE AS PERCENT OF VOTING AGE POPULATION	TURNOUT RATE AS PERCENT OF VOTING AGE PGPULATION
Syracuse, N. Y.	79.3	72.3
New Haven, Conn.	79.2	72.1
Kansas City, Kans.	78.9	66.4
Erie, Pa.	78.8	68.3
Philadelphia, Pa.	77.6	69.8
Sacramento, Calif.	77.3	66.4
Springfield, Mass.	77.1	67.0
Utica, N. Y.	77.1	76.1
Los Angeles, Calif.	77.0	64.2
Akron, Ohio	77.0	70.5
Toledo, Ohio	76.9	69.4
Trenton, N. J.	75.8	63.8
Elizabeth, N. J.	75.6	68.0
Santa Ana, Calif.	75.1	60.1
Rochester, N. Y.	74.9	72.2
Boston, Mass.	74.0	63.3
San Diego, Calif.	73.9	61.4
Cambridge, Mass.	73.8	65.9
Dayton, Ohio	73.6	62.5
Columbus, Ohio	72.4	63.1
Oakland, Calif.	71.9	66.2
Cleveland, Ohio	71.5	61.4
Winston-Salem, N. C.	71.2	50.5
Hartford, Conn.	70.7	34.1
Chattanooga, Tenn.	70.7	46.6
Bridgeport, Conn.	70.6	67.5
Charlotte, N. C.	69.9	54.5
St. Petersburg, Fla.	69.7	59.5
Tampa, Fla.	68.8	63.6
St. Louis, Mo.	68.5	62.0
Patterson, N. J.	68.4	55.4
Baltimore, Md.	68.1	54.0
San Francisco, Calif.	68.0	64.4
Niagara Falls, N. Y.	67.7	55.4
Allentown, Pa.	67.7	60.2
Greensboro, N. C.	66.6	52.6
Kansas City, Mo.	65.8	59.8
New York, N. Y.	65.7	58.8
Dallas, Texas	65.0	57.3
Baton Rouge, La.	64.7	47.8
Wichita, Kans.	62.2	43.0
Corpus Christi, Texas	61.8	53.9

TABLE 1.   Registration and Voting Rates in 104 Cities, 1960* (Continued)

CITY	REGISTRATION RATE AS PERCENT OF VOTING AGE POPULATION	TURNOUT RATE AS PERCENT OF VOTING AGE POPULATION
Newark, N. J.	61.4	50.4
Little Rock, Ark.	61.2	46.9
Honolulu, Hawaii	60.0	54.7
Houston, Texas	60.0	57.2
Miami, Fla.	59.2	43.7
Louisville, Ky.	59.0	32.4
Nashville, Tenn.	55.9	38.0
New Orleans, La.	55.6	45.9
Jacksonville, Fla.	54.9	46.9
Fort Worth, Texas	48.4	23.9
Austin, Texas	48.3	28.0
Richmond, Va.	46.5	31.2
Norfolk, Va.	43.6	22.4
San Antonio, Texas	42.6	31.4
Birmingham, Ala.	39.1	13.8
Portsmouth, Va.	38.0	25.7
Newport News, Va.	35.0	28.8
Atlanta, Ga.	33.8	25.6
Columbus, Ga.	32.1	24.2

* The list consists of all the cities in the U.S. with populations greater than 100,000 in 1960, with the following exceptions: registration figures were not available from 16 cities; similarly it was impossible to get accurate information concerning registration procedures for eight other cities.   For further discussion, see the original study.

rates were closely related to the turnout on election days in all the cities.   The table shows the cities ordered from highest to lowest registration rate.   As the table shows, the turnout figures generally followed the pattern of the registration figures quite closely, and the correlation between registration and voting was 0.88 (where 0.00 represents no linear association and 1.00 represents a perfect linear association).   Note also the pattern of the *differences* between cities; the authors report "if the percentage of the population of voting age registered to vote in city A was one percent higher than in city B, then the percentage of the population of voting age actually voting in city A was, on the average, almost exactly one percent higher than in city B."   This relationship held quite reliably for almost all of the 104 cities.   (See Figure 1, in which the data of Table 1 are plotted.)

Plainly those factors related to low turnout in cities might also be related to low registration rates.   But, in addition, does the nature of the registration procedure itself operate to limit the number of voters who register and, conse-

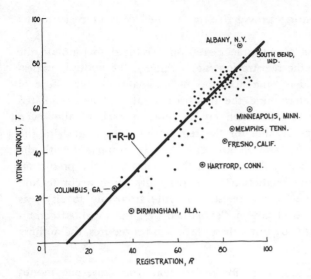

FIGURE 1

*City voting registration and
election-turnout percentages*

quently, to limit turnout?   The strong relationship between registration and turnout naturally suggests taking a careful look at factors that may produce the wide range of differences among cities.

The preceding discussion suggests three sets of forces determining the registration rate:

> *Factors affecting the value of the vote,* measured by
>   Closeness of recent elections
> *Factors affecting the costs of registration,* measured by
>   Closing date for registration
>   Provisions regarding literacy tests
>   Times and places of registration
> *Socioeconomic characteristics,* measured by
>   Age (percent who are 20 to 34)
>   Race (percent white)
>   Education (median school years completed by persons over 25 years
>   of age)

Each of the 104 cities was measured on each of these seven variables. Census data were used to determine the age, racial, and educational distribution of each city; the results of recent elections for President and Governor assessed the competiveness or closeness of elections; and information on the differing registration procedures provided data on the "costs of registration" in each city.

The statistical technique of multiple regression was used to estimate the impact of each variable on the registration rate. Simply, the multiple regression equation provides, under some assumptions, estimates of the effect of each of the variables in determining the registration rate. These estimated weights of impact, combined with each city's score on each of the seven variables, generate a predicted value for the registration rate of each of the 104 cities. This predicted registration rate can then be compared with the city's actual registration rate in order to assess the accuracy of the prediction equation. In this study, the predictions were generally quite accurate and most (80%) of the variation in the registration rate from city to city was described by, or in the statistical jargon, "explained by," the weighted combination of the seven variables. By using these statistical procedures, the authors concluded that

> (1) "Extending the closing date for registration from, say, one month to one week prior to election day would tend to increase the percentage of the population registered by about 3.6 percent." Thus the *convenience* of registration for the potential voter was strongly related to the rate of registration. It appears that in many cities political parties and politicians have manipulated the convenience of registration in order to decrease or increase the size of the electorate. This is, of course, a familiar story in some southern cities where Blacks have been prevented from registering to vote by means of violence, poll taxes, literacy tests, and other cumbersome and expensive registration procedures. Politicians and parties in the North, however, have also not been immune from designing registration procedures that have effectively prevented many citizens from voting. For example, one study found an almost perfect correlation between the ease of registration in different wards in a major city and the proportion of votes for that city's long-time incumbent mayor in the different wards.
>
> (2) The closeness or competitiveness of past elections was also strongly related to the registration rate: the closer the previous elections in the state, the more people registered to vote in the next election. Competitive elections not only offer the voter a greater range of plausible choices, but they also probably lead some voters to value their vote more than they would if elections were not close.
>
> (3) The various socioeconomic variables entered into the regression equation indicating that they, too, were associated with the registration rate. If a relatively large proportion of young people, Blacks, and families with less than average education lived in a city, then the registration rate in that city tended to be low.

CONCLUSIONS AND IMPLICATIONS

The results of the statistical analysis point to a number of important conclusions. The authors report that differences from city to city in participation in elections by the citizens were to a large extent related to registration rates, which, in turn, strongly reflected the local laws and practices regulating registration. Registration in some cities was made so difficult and so costly that fewer than one-third of the eligible voters ever registered to vote. In other cities, however, the ease of registration procedures, the competitiveness of elections, and certain socioeconomic factors resulted in more than 95% of the eligible citizens registering to vote. It is clear that many citizens were excluded from the polls because the costs of registering were too high for them to overcome. The elimination of restrictive and difficult registration requirements, both in the North and in the South, would increase political participation in the U.S. by reducing the costs of voting. Successful efforts to reduce the stringency of registration requirements would be far more effective in increasing voter turnout than exhortations by the mass media for citizens to go out and vote.

These suggestions, which grew out of the statistical study of registration and voting reported here, receive some further support from the experiences following the passage of the 1965 Voting Rights Act. Since the passage of the law, designed to simplify registration procedures and to reduce intimidation and other obstacles associated with registering in areas with low rates of registration, millions of citizens (both black and white) in the South now are registered and voting for the first time. In this political "experiment" the sudden reduction in the cost of registration led to sharp increases in political participation: prior to the law, less than 10% of the eligible citizens voted in some areas; now, in those same areas, 60% to 70% vote. No increases in registration and voting have been observed in areas not covered by the Voting Rights Act. Note that the theory that Americans are uniquely apathetic compared to the citizens of other democracies neither suggests remedies such as the Voting Rights Act nor explains the sudden upsurge in registration and voting in those areas covered by the Act. The experience with the new law, although certainly not representing a carefully controlled experiment, does at least provide some further independent evidence consistent with the results of the multiple regression study of registration and voting reported here.

The results also help to explain why turnout in elections in the U.S. is lower than in many other countries. Many democracies simply do not have voter registration procedures. (A few countries, in fact, even seek to increase the cost of *nonvoting* by means of compulsory voting.) Because a potential voter has to expend less time and energy to vote in democracies other than the U.S., it is not surprising that a great fraction of the citizens of other countries votes.   Roughly 80% of all potentially eligible voters register to vote in the U.S.   And about 80% of those registered actually do vote on election day—resulting in an overall turnout of around 64% of all potentially eligible voters.   In those countries (Canada, France, and Great Britain) with automatic registration requiring no effort on the part of the citizen, typically about 75% to 80% of all eligible citizens vote in national elections. Thus the persistently lower turnout in the U.S. is more likely due to inconvenient registration procedures than to any lack of civic virtue unique to Americans.

Finally, the findings in this statistical study of registration and voting suggest that nonvoting results from *political* factors as well as from socioeconomic factors.   Kelley, Ayres, and Bowen found evidence to support the conclusion that registration rules are manipulated by the party in power in order to make it easier for that party to continue to rule.   Thus, although nonvoting is related, in part, to persistent social conditions, it also often occurs because the dominant party has simply raised the inconvenience of voting to a high enough level so as to exclude many voters from the polls.

PROBLEMS

1.   What are the assertions that Kelley, Ayres, and Bowen set out to test in their study?

2.   Find Minneapolis on Table 1. What is its rank in voter registration? In voter turnout? What percentage of those registered actually voted?

3.   Suppose the voter registration and voter turnout rates in city i are R_i and T_i respectively. What is the range of *possible* values for T_i? [Answer: $0 \leqslant T_i \leqslant R_i$.]

4.   Consider Figure 1 where the relationship of registration and turnout is estimated. Suppose a city's registration was 75%. What is the predicted estimate of the city's turnout? Answer the same question for a city with 10% registration.

5.   What is the implicit procedure used by the author in deciding which cities to label in Figure 1?

6.   Can you think of other factors than those listed which might influence the voter registration rate? Explain why each of the factors you list might have an influence.

7.   For a given city in the sample, how do you assess the accuracy of prediction of the regression equation?

8.   Why does the author refer to the 1965 Voting Rights Act as a "political 'experiment' "?

9. True or false: The proportion of those who are registered to vote and actually do is roughly the same in the U. S. and Canada. Explain your answer.

REFERENCE

Stanley Kelly, Jr., Richard E. Ayres, and William G. Bowen. 1967. "Registration and Voting: Putting First Things First." *American Political Science Review* 61: June, pp. 359–379. Reprinted in Edward R. Tufte, ed. 1970. *The Quantitative Analysis of Social Problems.* Reading, Mass.: Addison-Wesley. Pp. 250–283.

PARKING TICKETS AND MISSING WOMEN: Statistics and the Law

Hans Zeisel   *University of Chicago*

Harry Kalven, Jr.   *University of Chicago*

THE LAW's traditional stance toward quantification and statistics was wittily expressed some years ago by one of its great professors, Thomas Reed Powell, who spoke of research in which thinkers don't count and counters don't think. By tradition, the concerns of the law have been qualitative and in large part based on the individual case; therefore, the thinker who would not count has been favored.

In recent decades, however, the law has shown some appetite for quantification, and we shall sketch some ways in which statistics has impinged on contemporary law.

PROOF BY DISPROOF OF COINCIDENCE

Perhaps the most striking use of statistics is to calculate the probability that a given event occurred by chance. The alternative explanation is that the event occurred by intent or another identifiable cause, and the recourse to statistics is to refute or support the contention that the matter was simply a coincidence.   Two examples are offered here, one simple, the other somewhat more complex.

Parking Tickets.   The simple example comes from a Swedish trial on a charge of overtime parking.   A policeman had noted the position of the valves of the front and rear tires on one side of the parked car, in the manner pilots note directions: one valve pointed, say, to one o'clock, the other to six o'clock, in both cases to the closest "hour" (see Figure 1).   After the allowed time had run out, the car was still there, with the two valves still pointing toward one and six o'clock.   In court, however, the accused denied any violation.   He had left the parking place in time, he claimed, but had returned to it later, and the valves just happened to come to rest in the same positions as before. The court had an expert compute the probability of such a coincidence by chance, the answer was that the probability is 1 in 144 (12×12), because there are 12 positions for each of two wheels.   In acquitting the defendant, the judge remarked that if all *four* wheels had been checked and found to point in the same directions as before, then the coincidence claim would have been rejected as too improbable and the defendant convicted; four wheels with 12 positions each can combine in 20,736 ($= 12 \times 12 \times 12 \times 12$) different ways, so the probability of a chance repetition of the original position would be only 1 in 20,736.   Actually, these formulas probably understate the probability of a chance coincidence because they are based on the assumption that all four wheels rotate independently of each other, which, of course, they do not.   On an idealized straight road all rotate together, in principle. It is only in the curves that the outside wheels turn more rapidly than the inside wheels, but even then the front and rear wheels on each side will presumably rotate about the same amount.   (See Zeisel 1968.)

FIGURE 1
Schematic diagram of parked car with valves at 1 and 6 o'clock

Missing Women. The second example arose from the 1968 trial of the pediatrician-author Dr. Benjamin Spock and others in the U.S. District Court in Boston for conspiracy to violate the Selective Service Act by encouraging resistance to the war in Vietnam. In that trial, the defense challenged the legality of the jury-selection method. Although more than half of all eligible jurors in Boston were women, there were no women on Dr. Spock's jury. Yet he, more than any defendant, would have wanted some because so many mothers have raised their children "according to Dr. Spock"; moreover, the opinion polls showed women in general to be more opposed to the Vietnam war than men.

The question was whether this total absence of women jurors was an accident of this particular jury or whether it had resulted from systematic discrimination. Statistical reasoning was to provide the answer.

In the Boston District Court, jurors are selected in three stages. The City Directory is used for the first stage; from it, the Clerk of the Court is supposed to select 300 names at random, that is, by a lotterylike method, and put a slip with each of these names into a box. The City Directory is renewed annually by censuslike household visits of the police, and it lists all adult individuals in the Boston area. The Directory lists slightly more women than men. The second selection stage occurs when a trial is about to begin. From the 300 names in the box, the names of 30 or more potential jurors are drawn. These people are ordered to appear in court on the morning of the trial. The subgroup of 30 or more is called a *venire.* In the third stage, the one that most of us think of as jury selection, 12 actual jurors are selected after interrogation by both the prosecutor and the defense counsel. Figure 2 shows the percentages of women in some 46 such venires selected by all seven judges of the Federal District Court in Boston.

The average proportion of women drawn by the six judicial colleagues of the Spock trial judge was 29%, and furthermore, the averages of these six judges bunched closely around the group average. This suggests that the proportion of women among the names in the 300-name panels in the jury box was somewhere close to that 29% mark. But Figure 2 shows also that the Spock judge's venires had consistently lower percentages of women, with an overall average of only 14.6% women, almost exactly half of that of his colleagues.

It is *possible,* of course, that the selection method used by the trial judge was the same as that of his six colleagues. But what is the probability that a difference as large (or larger) as that between 14.6 and 29% could arise by chance? Statistical computation revealed the probability to be 1 in 1,000,000,000,000,000,000 that the "luck of the draw" would yield the distribution of women jurors obtained by the trial judge or a more extreme one. The conclusion, therefore, was virtually inescapable: the venires for the trial judge

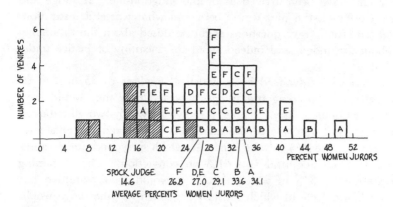

FIGURE 2

Number of venires by proportion of women (shaded blocks are for Spock judge venires; unshaded blocks are for other judges—A, B, C, D, E, F—of the Federal District Court in Boston). Averages are weighted by size of venire (not shown here). Source: Zeisel (1969)

must have been drawn from the central jury lists in a fashion that somehow *systematically* reduced the proportion of women jurors.

Thus the proportion of women among the potential jurors *twice* suffered an improper reduction—first, when the court clerk reduced their share from a majority in the City Directory to 29% in the jury lists and, second, when judge managed to lower the 29% to his private average of 14.6%. In the Spock trial, only one potential woman juror came before the court, and she was easily eliminated in stage 3 by the prosecutor under his quota of peremptory challenges (for which he need not give any reasons). (For further discussion see Zeisel 1969.)

ILLUMINATING DESCRIPTION

A second major use of statistics in the law is careful description. At times, it becomes relevant to measure, or at least to estimate within limits, some frequency, range, ratio, or level.   Three examples will be given.

Juries and Judges.   There has been perennial debate over the merits of the jury system, in particular over the differences between jury verdicts and the verdicts that would have been arrived at by the judge alone. If judge and jury hardly ever differed, the jury would be a somewhat wasteful institution; if they differed too often, grave questions might be raised about the rationality of the jury, about the judge, and indeed about the meaning of justice under law.

This debate has been advanced by a statistical analysis of 3576 criminal jury trials in which the presiding trial judges reported how they would have decided the case without a jury. Table 1 shows a two-by-two distribution that was a fundamental outcome of the analysis. The boxed percents refer to the 78% (=14% + 64%) of the trials in which jury and judge agree on the verdict, 14% on acquittal and 64% on conviction. The remaining 22% are disagreements: 3% in which the judge would have acquitted but the jury convicted, and 19% in which the jury acquitted but the judge would have convicted. Note, in particular, that for those cases in which the jury finds guilt, the judge agrees nearly all (96%) of the time, but for the cases in which the jury acquits, the judge agrees only about 42% of the time. Thus the jury tends to have a softening effect.

The figures fall into a range that approaches neither of the extremes; that is, the jury is not superfluous, nor do juries and judges disagree intolerably. If the reasons for the jury's disagreement turn out to be understandable, as indeed they do, the statistics offer basic insights into the viability of the jury as an institution. The range of reasons that move a jury to disagree with the judge is wide: a sense of justice concerning the particular crime that does not coincide with the letter of the law, a different view of the weight of the evidence, special attitudes towards the particular defendant, and so forth.

Quality of Counsel. Another such illumination of a heretofore dark corner pertains to how adequately defendants in criminal jury trials are represented

TABLE 1. Percent Agreement* and Disagreement Between Jury and Trial Judge (3576 Cases = 100%)

	JURY	
JUDGE	Acquitted	Convicted
Acquitted	14*	3
Convicted	19	64

Source: Kalven and Zeisel (1966).
* Boxed percents show agreement.

TABLE 2.   Quality of Counsel in Criminal Jury
Trials

	PERCENT
Defense counsel superior to prosecutor	11
Abilities equal	76
Prosecutor superior to defense counsel	13
Total	100
Number of Cases	(3576)

Source: Kalven and Zeisel (1966).

in the courts.   In recent years, there has been concern that all criminal defendants be represented at the various stages of the criminal process.   Less
attention has been paid to the quality of representation, although systematic
disparity would be a disturbing commentary on the basic fairness of our administration of justice.

The statistics in Table 2 summarize assessment by the presiding trial judges
mentioned above and are reassuring.

As we shall see below, inequality of counsel does affect the outcome of
the trial, so it is comforting to learn that in over three-fourths of the criminal
jury trials the ideal of the adversary system is realized: roughly equal cham-
pions on both sides.   It is also reassuring to learn that in the remaining
trials, the inequality goes in both directions about the same proportion of
times.   More complex questions might be raised about characteristics of the
defendants who recruit superior or inferior counsel, but we do not treat of them
here.

Automobile Injuries.   One more set of descriptive data, despite its simplicity,
provides insights and perspective on the functioning of a major part of the
legal system, this time the law of torts.   There is much debate these days
over how well the law works to compensate the victims of accidents, especially
automobile accidents.   A recent elaborate study of auto accidents in Michigan
revealed the distribution of reparations shown in Table 3.

The result may surprise those who assume that liability law is over-
whelmingly the most important source of compensation for accident victims.
As the figures indicate, this is no longer the case, and the importance of compensation from other sources suggests the feasibility of major legal reforms in the
direction of insured compensation for damages irrespective of fault on any-
body's part.   Several states have adopted, at this point, "no-fault" automobile
insurance.

TABLE 3.   Sources of Reparation for Automobile Injuries in Michigan, 1958

	PERCENT OF TOTAL DOLLARS
Liability of third parties who had negligently caused the accident (mostly insured some uninsured)	55
Injured's own insurance	
Accident	22
Hospital and medical	11
Life and burial	5
Social security	2
Employer and Workmen's Compensation	1
Other	4
Total	100% (= $85,196,000)

Source: Conrad et al. (1964, p. 63).

SAMPLING

The above examples depend mostly on sampling rather than censuslike operations, and in the study of legal as well as other institutions, sampling has enormously facilitated the possibilities of quantitative studies.

Sampling also has invaded the very core of the legal system, the fact-finding process in court trials and in hearings before administrative agencies. An important reason is that sampling can replace the cumbersome, and sometimes impossible, complete count or census. For example, a company's share of the consumer market may be determined by auditing a sample of stores, and the degree to which two competing trademarks are confused may be determined by interviewing a sample of consumers.

The rules of evidence that guide the courts and, to a lesser degree, the administrative agencies, have sometimes made it difficult to bring in sampling and survey data. If the data are collected through personal interviews, the rule against hearsay evidence, coupled with the guarantee of anonymity that is obligatory in most interviewing, may stand in the way. Sometimes the court simply distrusts sampling operations altogether. Thus, in a California case, a department store instituted suit for overpayment of local taxes, and submitted an estimate for the amount in question of $27,000, based on a sample of sales slips. The court insisted on the full count, only to discover that the correct amount was $26,750. On the whole, however, sampling operations have become more and more acceptable.

CAUSE AND EFFECT

The most complex use of statistics in law is measurement of the effect of particular rules or institutions. We conclude with two examples of this kind.

Pretrial Hearings. The first example comes from a controlled experiment, designed to reveal whether the worrisome number of cases requiring trial

TABLE 4. Obligatory Versus Optional Pretrial

	OBLIGATORY	OPTIONAL
Average length of trial time of the cases that reached trial	$8\frac{1}{4}$ hours	$7\frac{1}{4}$ hours
Percent cases not settled, hence reaching trial	24%	22%

Source: Rosenberg (1964).

is being reduced by the procedure known as pretrial hearing.   This is a hearing in which, prior to the trial proper, the litigants and their counsel are requested to appear before a judge to attempt to prepare the case so as to reduce the time required for its trial or to settle it there and then.

To learn whether pretrial hearings accomplish these aims, the state of New Jersey authorized an experiment: a random half of the filed suits were pretried as usual, but the other half were pretried only if one (or both) of the litigants requested it.   This happened only in 48% of this half of the cases.   The results of the experiment are summarized in Table 4. *Obligatory* pretrial achieved neither of its purposes and consumed court time, so the state of New Jersey decided to abolish it.

Effect of Counsel Quality.   As a final example, we shall discuss a survey that gauges the effect of superior counsel in criminal trials.   (A more detailed discussion appears in Kalven and Zeisel 1966.)

The survey data come from the real jury trials mentioned above; after each trial the presiding judge told us in confidence how he would have decided the case if it had been tried without a jury.   We use the judge's private decision as a base line against which to compare the jury, under the working assumption that the judge is far less affected by the skill of counsel than is the jury.   Table 5 summarizes the results of the survey.

The 88% in the upper left-hand corner of Table 5 has the following meaning: in those trials in which the judge would have acquitted and in which the defense counsel was superior to the prosecutor, the jury also acquitted

TABLE 5. Effects of Counsel Ability on Jury Verdicts in Criminal Cases

	DEFENSE COUNSEL SUPERIOR	ABILITIES EQUAL	PROSECUTOR SUPERIOR
Percent of cases where the judge would have *acquitted* that the jury acquitted	88%	82%	76%
Percent of cases where the judge would have *convicted* that the jury convicted	60%	78%	86%

Source: Kalven and Zeisel (1966).

in 88% of the cases.   (In the remaining 12%, the jury convicted, thus acting in disagreement with the judge's private conclusions.)   Moving one step to the right, we see that when the judge would have acquitted, but the defense counsel and prosecutor were equal in ability, the jury also acquitted less often, in 82% of the cases.   That is in conformance with intuition because for this group of cases we would expect the jury to be less swayed in the direction of acquittal by the skills of the defense counsel.   Moving one step more to the right, the 76% in the upper right shows that a superior prosecutor sways the jury away from acquittal by about the same amount that a superior defense counsel sways the jury toward acquittal (for cases in which the judge would have acquitted).   The arithmetic is direct: $88 - 82 = 6$, and $82 - 76 = 6$.

The bottom row gives analogous information for those cases in which the judge would have *convicted*.   When the defense counsel is superior, the jury also convicts in 60% of the cases; when the abilities are equal, the jury convicts more often, in 78% of the cases; when the prosecutor is superior, the jury convictions rise to 86%.   Here the changes in percent agreements with the judge are larger than before and unequal, 18% and 8%.

We note also what we saw earlier, that when the judge would have acquitted, the jury agreed with the judge more often than when the judge would have convicted.   For a symmetric comparison with respect to defense or prosecution superiority, it may be seen that 88% is greater than 86%, 82% greater than 78%, and 76% greater than 60%.

To temper the force of these estimates of counsel ability, it is useful to keep in mind Table 2, which showed that in most jury trials (76% of them) the quality of counsel on the two sides is about equal.   Hence the *overall* impact of superior counsel on the outcome of jury trials is modest.   Still, that is small consolation to the defendant with counsel of inferior ability who loses his particular case.

FINAL REMARKS

The foregoing examples illustrate the many ways in which statistics has begun to illuminate legal problems.   Yet this compact recital of examples should not leave the impression that the law is quick to appreciate the power of statistics.   On the contrary, statistics is only just beginning to enter the legal realm at rare and selected points.   It finds its most ready acceptance in the trial courts and before the administrative agencies, in litigation in which the issues depend on counting and measurement.   In constitutional adjudication and legislative action, however, the law typically states its issues in terms of principles that at least superficially appear to be less accessible to a statistical approach, but even here some progress is being made.   (See the essay by Alker.)

PROBLEMS

1. Assume the rear wheels of a car rotate independently of each other, while the front wheels rotate together. What is the probability of a person driving away from a space and returning to find all four valves pointing at the same "hours" as before departure?

2. What is meant by "proof by disproof of coincidence"?

3. What is the most frequent percentage of women jurors in a venire? (Give an approximate answer. Use Figure 2.)

4. In *Juries and Judges*, why do the authors say "the jury tends to have a softening effect"?

5. Referring to Table 1, what percentage of all cases were acquitted by the jury? Would have been acquitted by the judge?

6. Refer to Table 2. In how many cases were the lawyers of unequal ability?

7. How does Table 3 support a case for no-fault auto insurance?

8. What is sampling? Why is it sometimes difficult to use sampling and surveys as evidence?

9. Explain the experiment dealing with pretrial hearings. Why is this called a *controlled* experiment?

10. Suppose a second controlled experiment were conducted in which a random half of the filed suits were pretried as usual while the other half were not pretried. Suppose the results of this second experiment are given in the table.

Table. Pretrial Versus no Pretrial

	Pretrial	No Pretrials
Average length of trial time of cases that reached trial	6½ hours	8½ hours

Discuss the difference in design and results of the experiment reported here and the one reported in the text.

11. Refer to Table 5. Assume that the judge would have convicted in 100 cases, and that he felt 60% of the cases had lawyers of equal ability. The defense counsel was superior in half of the remaining cases. In how many cases did the jury acquit when the defense was superior?

REFERENCES

Alfred F. Conard et al. 1964. *Automobile Accident Costs and Payments*. Ann Arbor, Mich.: University of Michigan.

H. Kalven, Jr. and H. Zeisel. 1966. *The American Jury*. Boston: Little, Brown.

M. Rosenberg. 1964. *The Pre-Trial Conference and Effective Justice*. New York: Columbia.

H. Zeisel. 1968. "Statistics as Legal Evidence." D. L. Sills, ed., *International Encyclopedia of the Social Sciences*. New York: Macmillan.

H. Zeisel. 1969. "Dr. Spock and the Case of the Vanishing Women Jurors." *University of Chicago Law Review* 37:1–18.

H. Zeisel, H. Kalven, Jr., and B. Buchholz. 1959. *Delay in the Court*. Boston: Little, Brown.

ACKNOWLEDGMENTS

We wish to thank the following for permission to use previously published and copyrighted material:

Academic Press, for permission to adapt pp. 47–60 from Carl A. Bennet and Arthur A. Lumsdaine (Eds.) *Evaluation and Experiment: Some Critical Issues in Assessing Social Programs, 1975.*

Addison-Wesley Publishing Co., Inc., for permission to use the tables on pp. 81, 83, 87, and 88, from F. Mosteller and D. Wallace (1964), *Inference and Disputed Authorship.*

American Educational Research Association for permission to use Figure 3 on p. 31, from D. T. Campbell and J. C. Stanley (1963), "Experimental and Quasi-Experimental Design for Research on Teaching," in M. L. Gage, ed., *Handbook of Research on Teaching,* pp. 171–246.

American Psychological Association for permission to publish the figures on pp. 33 and 35 and Figure 9 on p. 36, from D. T. Campbell (1969), "Reforms as Experiments," *American Psychologist,* 24:4 (April), pp. 409–429. Copyright © American Psychological Association.

The College Entrance Examination Board for permission to publish the essay beginning on p. 11, which draws heavily upon William H. Angoff (1968), "How We Calibrate College Board Scores," *The College Board Review,* No. 68 (Summer).

Columbia University Press for permission to publish the table on p. 131 from M. Rosenberg (1964), *The Pre-Trial Conference and Effective Justice.*

The Law and Society Association for permission to publish the figures on p. 30 and Figure 10 on p. 36, from D. T. Campbell and H. L. Ross (1968), "The Connecticut Crackdown on Speeding: Time Series Data in Quasi-Experimental Analysis," *Law and Society Review,* 3:1, pp. 38, 42, 45.

Little, Brown and Company for permission to publish the tables on pp. 128, 129, and 131, from H. Kalven and H. Zeisel (1966), *The American Jury.*

New York City-RAND Institute for permission to publish the figures on p. 93, originally prepared for S. J. Press, report No. R-704.

Sage Publications, Inc., for permission to publish the figures on pp. 31 and 32, from H. L. Ross, D. T. Campbell, and G. V. Glass (1970), "Determining the Social Effects of a Legal Reform: The British 'Breath-alyser' Crackdown of 1967," *American Behavioral Scientist*, 13:4 (March/April), pp. 493–509.

University of Chicago Law Review for permission to publish the figure on p. 127, from H. Zeisel (1969), "Dr. Spock and the Case of the Vanishing Women Jurors," *University of Chicago Law Review*, 37, pp. 1–18.

University of Michigan Press for permission to publish the tables on p. 130, from Alfred Conrad et al. (1964), *Automobile Accident Costs and Payments*.

INDEX